Socio-Legal Philosophy of Bharat Ratna Dr B.R. Ambedkar

Socio-Legal Philosophy of Bharat Ratna Dr B.R. Ambedkar

(In the context of Weaker Sections of Society)

Dr Umakant N. Netragaonkar
M.A., LL.M., NET-in-Law;
NET-in-Criminology; P.C.C. (French);
M.D. (Dramatics) and Ph.D. (Law)

Ex-Incharge Principal
People's Education Society's Mumbai
Dr Ambedkar College of Law,
Nagsen Vana, Aurangabad - 431 001

Decent Books
New Delhi

Cataloging in Publication Data — DK
[Courtesy: D.K. Agencies (P) Ltd. <docinfo@dkagencies.com>]
Netragaonkar, Umakant N., 1959-
Socio-legal philosophy of Bharat Ratna Dr B.R. Ambedkar : in the context of
weaker sections / Umakant N. Netragaonkar.
p. cm.
Originally presented as the author's thesis (PhD) — Dr Babasaheb Ambedkar Marathwada University.
Bhimrao Ramji Ambedkar, 1891–1956, Indian statesman and social reformer.
Includes bibliographical references (p.).
ISBN 10: 8186921508
ISBN 13: 9788186921500
1. Ambedkar, B. R. (Bhimrao Ramji), 1891–1956. — Philosophy. 2. Social justice — India. 3. Equality before the law — India. 4. Dalits — Civil rights — India. I. Title.
DDC 303.372 095 4 22

ISBN 10: 81-86921-50-8 **ISBN 13: 978-81-86921-50-0**
First published in India in 2009
Second impression, 2012

Published and printed by:
Decent Books
D-36/A-1, Mohan Garden
Najafgarh Road
New Delhi - 110 059
Ph. (011) 2535 3435

Distributed by:
D.K. Printworld (P) Ltd.
Regd. Office: '*Vedaśrī*', F-395, Sudarshan Park
(Metro Station: Ramesh Nagar), New Delhi-110 015
Phones: (011) 2545 3975; 2546 6019; *Fax:* (011) 2546 5926
E-mail: dkprintworld@vsnl.net
Website: www.dkprintworld.com

Dedicated to my Parents

Shri Narsingrao Gundaji Netragaonkar
and
Smt. Jijabai Narsingrao Netragaonkar

in token of my gratitude towards them

Babasaheb Dr B.R. Ambedkar, the architect of Constitution of India, presenting copy of the Constitution to Dr Rajendra Prasad, the then President of India. Also in the picture: (l. to r.) Pandit Jawaharlal Nehru, Sardar Vallabhbhai Patal, Sri C. Rajagopalachari, Maulana Abul Kalam Azad. (Courtesy: Kaushalya Prakashan, N-11, C-3-24-3, HUDCO, Aurangabad - 431003)

Foreword

IT IS my privilege and great pleasure to contribute a foreword to this book of Shri Umakant Netragaonkar entitled *Socio-Legal Philosophy of Dr B.R. Ambedkar* in the context of weaker sections of Indian society. The title of this thesis itself is directly going to the root of the line of study of Babasaheb Ambedkar on various aspects by the writer. It is well known that Vishvabhushan Bharat Ratna Babasaheb Ambedkar is not only a towering personality but was also a mobile institution with numerous faculties. Babasaheb Ambedkar is the father of the Constitution of India, and he has experienced all the crises and problems, such as financial, social and religious, in his life. It is a known fact that Babasaheb Ambedkar was born in a depressed caste of the society. During those days his caste was totally discarded and known as "untouchable." The society of untouchables did not have any independent business, industry or employment. This caste was exclusively depending for its bread and butter on the so-called *savarna*s. Therefore, the economic conditions of these people were the worst. Similarly the religious division and the then traditional system of religion was in four tiers and Babasaheb Ambedkar was in the lowest tier of this caste system. He has experienced the gravity of untouchables based on the religious customs. Due to economic and religious disparity the social status was very miserable. Babasaheb Ambedkar devoted his entire life for the upliftment of social and economic conditions, and creation of awareness of the legal rights of the downtrodden and weaker sections of Indian society.

Shri U.N. Netragaonkar has categorically and minutely studied the thoughts of Babasaheb Ambedkar on social, economic and legal system and brought this knowledge to the common people. It is not limited to any particular caste. It is for the entire socio-economic weaker sections. The effort of Netragaonkar is worth appreciation and this book will definitely be a lamp-post showing a path to the students of Babasaheb Ambedkar's philosophy. Netragaonkar simplified the thinking and views of Babasaheb Ambedkar on social, economic and legal topics. This book will prove a useful guide for common people to chalk out a plan for bringing up the weaker sections to the competitive global level. The views expressed by Netragaonkar in this book will lay out a path with a vision to reach the ultimate goal of achieving the prosperity of weaker sections of society in India as envisaged by Babasaheb Ambedkar.

I am thankful to Netragaonkar for his hard work in the reproduction of the thoughts of Babasaheb Ambedkar on this subject with very simple and appropriate interpretations and making them available to the common man. This book should be helpful to all those devoted to the upliftment of the downtrodden people belonging to Scheduled Castes and Scheduled Tribes, and to those social workers who profess to be followers of Babasaheb Ambedkar's philosophy.

I wish him every success in his life.

C.L. Thool
Acting Chairperson
Maharashtra State Human
Rights Commission
9, Hazarimal Somani Marg
Opp. C.S.T. Railway Station
Mumbai - 400 001

24 January 2007

Preface

Bharat Ratna Dr Babasaheb Ambedkar: Messiah of the Downtrodden

Bharat Ratna Dr Bhimarao alias Babasaheb Ambedkar (1891-1956) was a messiah of the depressed classes, a noted jurist, the architect of India's Constitution, a profound scholar, an exceptionally daring social fighter, national leader and the greatest pioneer of Buddhist revival in India.

Throughout his life he struggled for the rights of the oppressed classes in society. He raised his voice against social inequality, injustice, suppression, exploitation and tyranny. His life's philosophy and mission were devoted to securing social justice and human rights for all in general and suppressed humanity in particular. His personality combines scientific thought and bold action. He appealed to the depressed classes to "Educate, Organize, and Agitate" and to forge ahead on the basis of self-defence, self-dignity and self-help.

Dr Ambedkar had realized the importance of education as a crucial weapon for bringing about social transformation and upliftment of the depressed classes. He founded the Peoples Education Society and Siddharth College in Mumbai in 1945. In the year 1950 Dr Ambedkar founded Milind Mahavidyalaya, which was the first full-fledged degree college in Nagsenvana, Aurangabad, and had the foundation stone laid by India's first President Dr Rajendra Prasad, in the presence of His Excellency the Nizam of Hyderabad State.

Milind Mahavidyalaya was loved as a petchild by Dr Ambedkar who spent a number of years on its campus and nourished and brought up the Institution. During the course of time Peoples Education Society opened new schools, colleges and hostels at various places.

Dr Ambedkar was having a versatile personality, and being a great thinker and philosopher, he founded several social, religious, and educational organizations for the promotion of social equality and to inspire the eminent intellectuals on a social mission.

In order to study the social, economic, educational, cultural and ethnic conditions prevailing in the society and to provide solutions for their problems Ambedkar sought the views of eminent scholars and writers. He being a great journalist he founded the newspapers and weeklies like *Muknayak, Bahishkrut Bharat, Janata* and *Prabuddha Bharat.* Nothing gives an author greater satisfaction than the acceptability of his writing by those for whom he writes.

In the present text an honest attempt has been made to simplify, to the extent possible, the socio-legal philosophy of Dr Ambedkar, which is inherently a manifold subject. The basic themes of the philosophical thoughts of Ambedkar on the subjects of social, political, economical, religious and constitutional legacy have been analyzed in simple language without diluting the essence of his philosophy. The author does not regard that the present work is the entire socio-legal philosophy or an exhaustive analytical work, but merely a humble attempt as brain tonic to the requirement of the students, teachers, scholars, judges, advocates, social workers and those who serve humanity.

The thoughts of Dr Babasaheb Ambedkar are of immense value like the sparks of diamonds. Such a book is essential for knowing his views in his own words. The thoughts are studied with gems of historic facts, basic values and exalted vision.

I am sure that, these exhortations will inspire and guide scholars, writers, speakers as well as the common man and will certainly help the society to change according to the times.

I feel this text exposes the readers to the gems that lie scattered in the form of the immortal writings of one of the great intellectuals of the twentieth century Bharat Ratna Dr Babasaheb Ambedkar. The present book is a collection of the choicest gems which should serve as the beacon light guiding our thoughts and efforts in ushering a new socio-economic order affording dignity and justice to every human being.

I am sure that this text will provide vision of a new social order which hopefully will fulfil the dreams and aspirations of India's teeming millions.

In the present book I have discussed the philosophical thoughts of Dr Ambedkar in seven chapters. The introductory part explains definitions of philosophy, and various aspects and approaches of Dr Ambedkar towards social, economic, political, religious and Constitutional issues.

In chapter 1 I have discussed social background and new era of Buddhist philosophy and its influence on Indian history. Ashoka made Buddhism the religion of the State. This was of course a great blow to Brahmanism. Brahmanism lost all patronage and it was relegated to a secondary position in the empire of Ashoka. Caste and castiest attitude. Untouchability is a leprosy of Hinduism and it should be eradicated through law. Therefore special provisions had been introduced by Ambedkar in the Indian Constitution.

Economic philosophy, i.e. general problems of Economics, Evolution of Provincial Finance of the East India Company,

Economy and Globalization. Economic Reforms. Small Holdings in India and their remedies, silent features of Socialism, Landless Labour, Employment and Industrial Relations are several aspects which have been discussed in chapter 2.

In Chapter 3 Dr Ambedkar's contribution to social justice have been discussed. He was determined to bring revolutionary changes in the national life of India. We all know that in India there existed a traditional social set-up which was held under the tentacles of caste-ridden inequality for centuries together. It was like a pond of stagnant water. Dr Ambedkar wanted to bring a complete change in social, economic and political life of the Indian society. He experienced that millions of people were deprived of even basic human rights. He fought relentlessly for their rights till his last breath and succeeded in securing them. Social justice was the cornerstone of his movement. He was the harbinger of human rights. (Foreword page xii, para no. 2, *Dr Babasaheb Ambedkar Writings and Speeches*, vol. 17, part 1).

He believed that democracy was not only a form of government, but it was essentially a form of society. He wanted a society based on democratic values. He gave a gallant fight against orthodoxy to obtain these rights. He is the pioneer of democracy in India. The Constitution is the core of our national life. He always insisted upon egalitarian society. It was his conviction that political, social and economic changes can be brought about only through constitutional means. (Ibid., page no. xi, para no. 3).

Unlike other great thinkers of the world, Dr Ambedkar was not an abstract thinker. He participated actively in political and social activities. Being the Chairman of the Drafting Committee, he burned the midnight oil to draft our

Constitution. Through this Constitution, he endowed human rights to all those who were exploited and deprived of the basic rights. During his tenure as a Labour Minister his work for the upliftment of labour class was invaluable and unparalleled. (Ibid., page no. xii, para no. 4).

Dr Ambedkar's life is a saga of relentless struggle against the orthodox society. The society was based on the impregnable citadel of conservatism, inequality, injustice and exploitation. His approach was based mainly on social justice. He proved to be the liberator and saviour for the millions of Indian people. He believed that his countrymen would some day realize that the country is always greater than the person. (Ibid., page no. xiii, para no. 2).

This volume envisages his vital role in nation building. He was associated with all the historical events like South Borough Commission, Simon Commission, Round Table Conference, 1935 Act, Cripps Mission, Cabinet Mission etc. He proved his mettle in drafting the revolutionary document, i.e. "Constitution of India". The Constitution has been hailed by many great statesman and scholars. They see the Constitution as the foremost social document. Through this Constitution he laid down the foundation of democracy. It was his conviction that economic democracy should be strengthened with social and political democracy. Ambedkar emphasized on national integration and secularism. Without social union political unity is difficult to be achieved. If achieved, it would be as precarious as a summer sapling liable to be uprooted by the gust of hostile wind. (Ibid., page no. 11, para no. 3).

Therefore I have tried to provide important thoughts under the subheads: Dr Ambedkar's Contributon to Emancipation and Development of SCs, Promotion of Interests of Minorities, Improvement of position of Women, and Betterment in the Condition of Labour.

In chapter 4 discussion has been focussed on historical background of the Indian National Congress and Hindu Mahasabha and their attitude towards removal of untouchability till the framing of the Constitution of India. Ambedkar submitted a memorandum in which he asserted that the political and economic safeguards for the SCs and STs should be guaranteed in the Constitution and their representation to be made on the basis of their population. He prepared separate electorates for the untouchables. Article 16 gives an assurance of equality of opportunity in public employment. According to Article 16(4) the State will not be prevented from making any provision for the reservation of appointment in favour of any backward class of citizens, which in the opinion of the State is not adequately represented in the services under the State. Dr Ambedkar placed considerable emphasis on creating an educated middle class which might have great potential for exacting social reforms. (Ibid., pages 116, 117, para no. 2).

The Constitution makes an earnest attempt at removing untouchability. Article 17 of the Constitution provides that untouchability stands removed, and its practice in any shape or form has been made a punishable offence. An attempt has been made to trace out the efforts made by the Indian National Congress and Ambedkar to abolish untouchability. No doubt, the growth of the Indian democratic system was to rest on the principle of equality. The principle is artistically fused with Articles 14, 15, 16, 29(2), 44, 325 and 326. (Ibid., page no. 117, para no. 3).

During his tenure as Prime Minister, V.P. Singh announced in Parliament on 9th August 1990 his decision to reserve certain percentage (27%) of all government jobs for "Backward Classes." The nine member Constitution Bench of the Supreme Court of India delivered its historic judgment in the Reservation case related to Socially and Educationally Backwards Classes (SEBCs) popularly known as "Mandal Case" on 16th November 1992. There are several other cases discussed by the Supreme Court of India. These judgments opened the mind of the judges in respect of equality before law, equal protections and reservation policy in the focus of the Constitutional mandatory provisions. (Ibid., page no. 1).

Chapter 5 is focussed on Dr Ambedkar's views on Article 356 of the Constitution of India. Dr Ambedkar throughout his life fought for the protection of human rights of women, particularly down-trodden, suppressed and oppressed persons in general and those who were thrown into darkness for thousands of years by the traditional high-caste Hindu orthodoxy. His approach was not just concerned with matters of political strategy; it is also important to consider the deeper implication of the distinction between the fight for rights and fight for values. (para no. 2 of the text page 135).

Values represent the framework within which demand for rights is negotiated. Sometimes there may be good reasons, sometimes there may not be. Values play a very crucial role in the social validation of rights. (para no. 2 of the text page 136).

Once, Katju, the Home Minister angrily snubbed Dr Ambedkar, "you made the constitution." And Ambedkar's reply was a rare specimen of frankness. "I was a hack, what I was to do, I did much against my will." (H.M. Seervai, *Constitutional Law of India* vol. 2, pp. 2624-29).

Chapter 6 sheds light on Dr Ambedkar and weaker sections of the society. To Dr Ambedkar adoption of a new religion becomes inevitable, which is fair and reasonable and ensures a place of honour and dignified living. Where a religion discriminates and confers no status, naturally a man would like to seek conversion to another religion which would save him from atrocities and exploitation and guarantee him a life like all others. (para 1, text p. no. 150).

To Ambedkar "democracy" refers to fundamental changes in the social and economic life of the people and acceptance of those changes by the people without resorting to dispute and bloodshed. (Extracts from para no. 2 of the text page 158).

"Painfully conscious of the social and economic inequalities which *corroded* the national consciousness of the Indian people, he unrelentingly desired to remove the contradictions created by economic and social inequalities. He wanted to establish the principles of one man-one vote and one vote and one value not only in the political life in India but also in its social and economic spheres." (extracts from para no. 3 of the text page 158).

"What we need today is one single caste of humanity, one common religion of love, and one universal language of heart. No society can find its fulfilment, no social ideal can fructify without the blossoming of the spirit of man." (extracts from para no. 2 of the text page 176).

Court justice and social justice in India according to Ambedkar is the focus of chapter 7.

C.J. Friedrich concludes that even if justice be seen merely in terms to accord with prevalent values three absolute criteria are inherent in it. Those are: (i) truth of the basing affects, (ii) non-arbitrariness — relating the basing facts to values, and (iii) non-performance of the norms derived. (extracts from para no. 2 of the text page 184).

Social Justice and Constitution: The Constitution of India in the preamble resolved to secure for all its citizens: Justice: Social, Economic and Political. Therefore the concept of justice is not foreign to legal order. Social justice is the primary objective of the State envisaged by our Constitution (extracts from para no. 3 of the text page no. 186).

I hope, this book will be most useful not only to the students of law but also to those who are interested to study the thoughts of Dr Ambedkar.

I am grateful to several authors, learned scholars, also government and non-government agencies whose writings have provided me insight into cases of the subject.

Aldous Huxley remarked that, "A bad book is as much a labour to write as a good one, it comes sincerely from the author's souls." I shall consider my efforts to have been rewarded if the book could be helpful to whom it is meant for.

I will be glad to receive comments and suggestions in particular from the students' community for the improvements of the contents of this treatise.

I crave the indulgence for any errors or imperfection which might have, despite the care and caution taken, crept in this book.

14/4/2009

Dr Umakant N. Netragaonkar

Samrat Niwas
N-2, M-2, 10/4, CIDCO Ram Nagar,
Jalna Road (Airport Road)
AURANGABAD - 431 003 (Maha.)
Ph: 0240-247 0490, Mob: 093250 37083

Contents

Acknowledgement

It is my great pleasure and special thanks to the Hon'ble C.L. Thool, Acting Chairman, Human Rights Commission, Maharashtra State, who had written Foreward to this book. I express my sincere thanks to my research guide Late Dr Vishnu Egaonkar who was guide for legal research at the initial stage. Thereafter Dr Balasaheb Bharaswadkar guided me to complete my research work. My special thanks to Dr A. Laxminathan, Vice-Chancellor, Arya Chanyak National Law University, Patna (the then Registrar, National Law University, Nalasar, Hydrabad and Prof. Shirish Deshpande, Law Department, Nagpur University, Nagpur, who acted as referee for Ph.D. viva voce and both of them encouraged me for writing the present book.

I am always in debt to my parents, both of them gave me encouragement for writing this book. I am also thankful to my family members Mrs. Chandrakala and my sons Kanchanjeet, Pankajkumar, Chandankumar and Anandkumar for their helping hands from time to time and for their kind co-operation.

I also express my thanks to our college students, staff members and my friends Prof. Dr A.C. Ahire, Prof. More, Prof. Shashikant Shirsath, Prof. Mrs. Bhagyashree Paranjape (Godbole) and Adv. Rajendra Godbole, Adv. Shivajirao Shinde, Adv. Sharma, Dr V.L. Dharurkar and all other known and unknown persons who have given me encouragement for writing this book.

My special thanks to Mr Rajendra Agarwal, Publisher, and all staff members of Decent Books, New Delhi, who have published this book within a short span of time and made available to the readers.

Dt. 14/4/2009 **Dr Umakant N. Netragaonkar**

Introduction

SOCIAL Justice movement was one of the important characteristics of twentieth-century philosophical schools. Bharat Ratna Dr B.R. Ambedkar both as a scholar and philosopher was a crusader for establishing social justice to Dalits and weaker sections of Indian society. Here in order to study his contribution to socio-legal philosophy, the vision of Ambedkar for the upliftment of Dalits must be carefully studied in a socio-legal perspective. He was able to make a well organized intellectual attack against the outdated caste system of Indian society. In order to complete the unfinished task of Ambedkar, reviewing his ideas on socio-legal philosophy would be most relevant to face global challenges. Ambedkar was the first Indian scholar who analysed the role of caste and religion in Indian society in a critical manner.

According to S.N. Choudhary,

> Ambedkar pleaded for the annihilation of caste. But today because of various reasons the caste system, as tradition, has modernized some of its traits by widening its areas of activity.[1]

In order to curb the situation we will have to understand the progressive ideas of Dr Babasaheb Ambedkar in the realm of socio-legal philosophy.

---

1. S.N. Choudhary "Ambedkar, Caste and Hindu Religion: An Analysis," *Ambedkar and Social Justice* in S.S. Shashi ed., New Delhi: Publication Division, GOI, 1992, vol. I, p. 137.

Dr Babasaheb Ambedkar was a critic of caste system. He had pointed out that:

> Caste in the hands of the orthodox has been a powerful weapon for prosecuting the reforms and for killing all reforms. Caste is the monster that crosses your path. You cannot have economic reform unless you kill this monster.[2]

In view of this we have to study the original ideas of Dr Babasaheb Ambedkar. He said that:

> the caste system is opposed to development and unity in the wider sense but I am afraid to submit whether the same may be advocated by those Harijans who get benefit of various types because they belong to a particular caste. What I am to submit is that with different degree all the castes and sub-castes are functionally related to the caste system, and the latter can only be abolished when a suitable alternative is searched out and as pre-conditions are available.[3]

In order to understand the supreme value of Dr Babasaheb Ambedkar's philosophy, we have to examine his contributions in a critical sense. The relevance of Dr Babasaheb Ambedkar's socio-legal philosophy in current global situation in general, and Indian conditions in particular, is highly significant because the modern societies are going through disparity and imbalance at different levels. A more precise and sharp analysis of his legal philosophy can be useful to relieve tensions prevailing at all levels.

The concept of philosophy has been defined by many scholars. The *Oxford English Dictionary* defines philosophy as

---

2. Ibid., p. 7.
3. Ibid., p. 137.

"the love, study or pursuit of wisdom or knowledge of things and their causes, whether theoretical or practical."[4]

According to Bertrand Russell,

> A critical examination of the grounds for fundamental beliefs and an analysis of the basic concepts employed in the expression of such beliefs.[5]

We have to understand Dr Babasaheb Ambedkar's socio-legal philosophy since such a viewpoint is highly required.

What is Philosophy?

The most universal concept of human thought, in its urge for more and more clarification, always stands in need of definition. The philosopher has constantly to reflect on these concepts till they are mature enough to interpret the Reality corresponding to them, with the utmost approximation. Besides logical analysis, such a reflection is based on the meaning of the concept which, in its turn, is related to experience to which it corresponds. Thus, in the ultimate analysis, to define any concept the philosopher must proceed with the double process of logical analysis of the concept and critical reflection on the experience for which it stands. The philosopher in his synoptic vision would only point out the broad and general characteristic of a particular concept. Obviously, a definition of philosophy would not define this or that philosophy but philosophy in general.

Introduction to Philosophy

We are proceeding with a twofold process of logical analysis of the concept and a critical survey of the historical treatment of the subject.

---

4. *The Oxford English Dictionary*, vol. VIII, London, 1933, p. 781.
5. *Webster's Third New Dictionary*, 1938, vol. II, p. 1698.

As a general rule, the history of philosophy is a collection of the reasoned interpretation of the experiences of the individuals representing different aspects of Truth. Hence, what is desirable is not a destructive criticism of other approaches, but the assessment of their values on the whole and to find in it a reasonable place for each of them.

Historical Reviev

Aristotle devised Metaphysics to be studied after physics. Thus etymologically speaking, metaphysics means "after-physics." It is the last science, the science, the science of science. It is also the first science, the mother of all sciences. He also calls it the science of being though such a science is impossible since science deals only with process of phenomena. Philosophy deals with Becoming. Thus it includes sciences within its ken. Man experiences eternity as well as change. Philosophy is an explanation of the total experience of man who seeks the integral truth.

The rationalists in the early dawn of modern philosophy defined metaphysics as a knowledge deduced from self-evident principles. This attempt at rationalisation or mathematisation of philosophy sought to make it more exact. But metaphysics with thought as its instrument should never dream of being exact like mathematics since thought, though real, cannot be identified with Reality. To be inexact is both a weakness as well as the strength of metaphysics. The philosopher is a lover of knowledge and never a sole possessor of it. The complete comprehension of Infinite by Finite is a logical impossibility and yet the destiny of man lies in progressing for an ever near approximation to it.

Human thought which always bifurcates Reality into form and essence, subject and object, "that" and "what" can never truly represent the Reality which is an all-inclusive spiritual unity. Philosophy is not a matter of logico-mathematical deduction or induction. The laws of Geometry are not applicable to Metaphysics any more than they are applicable to Chemistry of Physiology. Every new field of experience has its own laws. Philosophy, the moment it loses touch with immediate experience of Reality, forgets its way in the wilderness of human ratiocination which leads us nowhere.

The necessity of basing philosophy on experience was loudly proclaimed by the opposite school of empiricists represented by Locke, Berkeley and Hume. Locke pointed out that for its content the form and instrument of metaphysics is dependent on experience. This was a great corrective to rationalistic extreme and yet by confining metaphysics to mere sense experience, the empiricists shifted the balance in the opposite direction which led to the negation of all metaphysics. This is obvious, since if sense experience is the only experience, philosophy is a mere wild goose chase.

To be itself, philosophy should widen its field to include all types of experience, religious, moral, scientific, spiritual, etc. **Hume** defined the supremacy of Reason. But if reason is a slave to passion, the refutation of reason, being itself a ratiocination, stands self-condemned. Hume's "criticism of rationalism and reduction and absurdum of empiricism," however, gives a lesson which philosophy should not forget. Reason is its surest instrument but to get its data, it should rely on experience.

Kant combines the Beconian idea of the extension of knowledge with the Cartesian idea of certainty. But he also fights shy of all metaphysics in the ultimate sense. Only the metaphysics of Nature and metaphysics of knowledge are possible. Thus, it was left to **Hegel** to revive in full vigour the ultimate status of philosophy. The object of philosophy, according to him, is to search out the concept, the purpose, the significance of phenomena and to assign to these their corresponding positions in the world and in the system of knowledge. It systematises a true view of Philosophy as a systematisation of values and facts. But, by the identification of Nature with Logic Hegel arrives at an intellectualism which led **Bradley** to assert with a vengeance, "Metaphysics is the finding of bad reasons for what we believe on instinct."

This curt remark is a timely warning to all those who attempt at reduction to Reality of mere thought but the rejection of all metaphysical speculation as bad reasons appears to be too sweeping. The intellect is not rejected in Spirit but transformed into a better instrument to receive the truth.

Bergson's approach here seems to be more balanced than that of Bradley. Philosophy, according to him, must take into account not only sensory but also mental and intuitive experiences. It must be based on Real experience. Bergson shows a true insight into the problem when he points out that the difference between various schools of philosophy is because of their fragmentary glimpse of Reality, supplemented by different kinds of intellectual interpretation and elaboration. He suggests that by mutual comparison and elimination of peculiarities, philosophers may grasp the universal character of basic Reality.

Again, philosophy according to Bergson "does not only facilitate speculation; it give us also more power to act and live. For with if we feel ourselves no longer isolated in humanity, humanity no longer seems isolated in the Nature that it dominates." Finally Bergson said, "in its usual capacity in practical life intellect works on data supplied by sense-perception. Otherwise, the intellect may co-operate with intuition by assembling the data of intuition and forming fluid concepts. Intuition and reason are equally indispensable instruments of Philosophy."

Contemporary thought witnesses a chaos in the field of Metaphysics. All sorts of arguments have been advanced to support widely divergent views of Reality. All kinds of reactions are raising their heads under big-sounding names of "isms." All types of methods have been put to test. The purpose of Nature beneath all this burning cauldron of ideologies, however, seems to be the manifestation of an integral philosophy which may reconcile all and transcend all, and rouse itself from its dogmatic slumber. A true philosophy is the intellectual search for the fundamental truth of things.

It is generally agreed by all that philosophy must be based on experience but as we have already seen, often the term experience has been limited to certain specific regions. The root fallacy underlying all the conflicting schools of philosophy is a shift from the centre to periphery, an exaltation of part as whole, a dogmatic denial of everything beyond the limited ken of intellect and finally, an unwarranted application of the logic of finite to the matters of the Infinite. "The work of philosophy" as **Sri Aurobindo** rightly points out, "is to arrange the data given by the various means of knowledge, excluding none, and put them in synthetic relation to the one truth, the one supreme and universal reality."

Philosophy should be all-comprehensive, affirmative, synthetic and spiritual. Philosophy, meaning love of wisdom (philos=love, sophia=wisdom) should be distinguished from mere opinion. Knowledge, as the Indians conceived it, is the knowledge of that by knowing which everything else can be known. Thus philosophy is the knowledge of Ultimate Reality. But Ultimate Reality, as Indian philosophy truly maintains, is not only Existence but also Consciousness and Bliss. Hence, philosophy, as the quest after ultimate truth, is science of value *par excellence*. It should not only criticise facts but also satisfy religion and science. To quote Sri Aurobindo, "It should be a discovery of the real reality of things by which human existence learns its law and aim and the principle of its perfection."

Definition of Philosophy

A beginner in philosophy is perturbed to find that different philosophers have given different definitions of philosophy. While some philosophers have laid emphasis on psychological facts, others have given more importance to values. According to **John Dewey,** "Whenever philosophy has been taken seriously, it has always been assumed that it signified achieving a wisdom that would influence the conduct of life."

On the other hand, according to **Windelband,** philosophy is ". . . the critical science of universal values." While there is much difference in Indian and Western definitions of philosophy, one finds widely different definitions presented by Western philosophers also. Of these definitions some emphasize the critical aspect of philosophy while others lay emphasis upon its synthetic aspect. Some examples of these two types of definitions of philosophy are as follows:

Philosophy is a critical method of approaching experience. Examples of this type of definition are as follows:

> Philosophy is essentially a spirit or method of approaching experience rather than a body of conclusion about experience. — ***Egar S. Brightman***

> It is not the specific content of these conclusions, but the spirit and method by which they are reached, which entitles them to be described as philosophical . . . — ***Clifford Barrat***

> Were I limited to one line for my answer to it, I should say that philosophy is a general theory of criticism.
>
> — ***C.J. Ducasse***

Philosophy is comprehensive synthetic science. The following definitions of philosophy emphasize its synthetic aspect:

> Philosophy like science, consists of theories of insights arrived at as a result of systematic reflection.
>
> — ***Joseph A. Leighton***

> Philosophy is concerned with everything as a universal science. — ***Herbert Spencer***

> Our subject is a collection of sciences, such as theory of knowledge, logic, cosmology, ethics and aesthetics, as well as a unified survey. — ***Roy Wood Sellars***

The above-mentioned definitions of philosophy show that while some philosophers have mainly emphasized critical philosophy, others have defined it as a synthetic discipline. In fact both these viewpoints are one-sided because philosophy is both critical as well as synthetic. Literally speaking, the word "philosophy" involves two Greek words — **"Philo"** meaning love and **"Sophia"** meaning knowledge. Thus literally speaking, philosophy means love of wisdom. It should be noted here that the definition of philosophy is different from the sense in which the word "Darshan" has been taken in India. The literal meaning of philosophy shows that the philosopher is constantly and everywhere engaged in the search for truth. He does not bother so much to arrive at final conclusions and continues with his search for truth throughout his life. His aim is the pursuit of truth rather than its possession. Those who enjoy journey do not care so much about the destination, neither are they perturbed when the destination is lost in sight in spite of continued long journey.

In an effort to define philosophy, one arrives at the difficulty that there is no genus in this case and also no differentia. In defining a science one points out to the genus science and also to the particular area of the particular science which differentiates it from others. This is however, not possible in the case of philosophy because philosophy is one and not many. Hence in order to arrive at the meaning of philosophy you will have to discuss its problems, attitude, method, process, conclusions and results. In brief, philosophy is a philosophical process of solving some characteristic problems through characteristic methods, from a characteristic attitude and arriving at characteristic conclusion and results. Some might find this definition very vague and inadequate. But while defining science, do we not say that science is scientia or that it is a method, and can we understand this definition of science without understanding scientific method? When science cannot be understood without knowing scientific method, how can we hope to understand philosophy without knowing philosophical method? Again, in understanding the definition of science we are required to understand not only scientific problems and scientific conclusions because all these together form a science. Therefore, what is vague and inadequate if we say that in order to understand philosophy one must understand the attitude, problems, activity, conclusions and results peculiar to it? This will also clarify the distinction between philosophy and science which has been forgotten by many philosophers.[6]

Philosophy has been defined by many scholars in distinct ways. It has been pointed out that,

> philosophy is the term the meaning of which has in the course of centuries undergone considerable modifications.[7]

6. *Rajiv Tiwari, "Philosophy"* Delhi : Manoj Publications, pp. 7-28.
7. *Twenty-first Century Universal Encyclopedia*, vol. 22, p. 275.

According to Sturt Hampshire,

> philosophy means a quest for truth through logical reasoning rather than factual observation. Every advance in knowledge robs some problems which formerly it had.[8]

Here we are trying to explore the socio-legal philosophy of Ambedkar in a critical manner.

Legal philosophy is also an important and developing school of modern philosophy. Ambedkar as a socio-legal philosopher needs an independent and careful treatment. Harris has rightly described the concept of legal philosophy. He has pinpointed that,

> legal philosophy means that branch of practical philosophy which investigates the value implication of describing something as legal.[9]

Ambedkar himself has described the need of social justice in a systematic manner. He has observed that, "If you ask me my ideal it would be a society on liberty, equality and fraternity."

An ideal society should be mobile and full of channels for conveying a change taking place in one part to other parts.[10]

This ideal can be achieved through a positive angle. He had traced back his roots of philosophy from Buddhism.He had noted that,

> positively, my social philosophy may be said to be enshrined in three words: Liberty, Equality, and Fraternity. Let no one

---

8. *Webster's Third New Dictionary*, op. cit., p. 1698.
9. J.W. Harris, *Legal Philosophies*, London: Butterworth, 1980, p. 5.
10. Compiled by N.G. Kamble, K.M. Kamble, M.L. Kasare, *Essentials of Dr B.R. Ambedkar*, Nagpur: Social Forum Publications, 1991, p. 15.

> however say I borrowed my philosophy from the French Revolution, I have not. My philosophy has roots in religion and not in political science. I have derived them from the teaching of my Master, the Buddha.[11]

This tradition shows his Indian viewpoint. Further he had believed that,

> our aim is to realize in practice our ideal of one man one value in all walks of life — political, economic, and social.[12]

He believed in the principle of equality and he had pointed out that,

> if all these communities are to be brought to the level of equality, then the only remedy is to adopt the principle of inequality and to give favoured treatment to those who are below the level.[13]

Such a passion for equality was his mission. He was a truthful philosopher, who had explored these facts in a nutshell. He had noted that,

> without social union, political unity is difficult to be achieved. It would be as precarious as summer sapling, liable to be uprooted by the gust of hostile wind.[14]

Ambedkar was a champion of legal society. About the philosophy, he had observed that,

> rights are protected not by law but by the social and moral conscience of society. If social conscience is such that it is prepared to recognize the rights which law chooses to enact, then rights will be safe and secure.

---

11. Ibid.
12. Ibid.
13. Ibid.
14. Ibid.

> But if the fundamental rights are opposed by community, no law, no parliament and no judiciary can guarantee them in the real sense of the word.[15]

There was clarity and validity in his legal philosophy. In the domestic society he observed that,

> the first is an attitude of mind, an attitude of respect and equality towards their fellows. The second is a social organization free from rigid social barriers. Democracy is incompatible and inconsistent with isolation and exclusiveness resulting in the distinction between the privileged and the unprivileged.[16]

This changing attitude is mostly essential to bring domestic way of life. There is a need to bridge the gap in our society. He further pointed that,

> looking to the problem from the materialistic point of view, the surest way for their salvation lies in higher education, higher employment and better ways of earning a living. Once they become well placed in the scale of social life, they would become respectable; and once they become respectable, the religious outlook of the orthodox towards them is sure to undergo a change. Even if this does not happen, it can do no injury to their material interests.[17]

Ambedkar moved on to say that we should change the outlook of weaker sections. His ideas were on social support. He had opined that,

> when the social reformer challenges society, there is nobody to hail him a martyr. There is nobody even to befriend him. He is loathed and shunned. But when the political patriot

---

15. Ibid.
16. Ibid., p. 16
17. Ibid., p. 15

> challenges government he has the whole society to support him. He is praised, admired and elevated as the saviour. Who shows more courage: the social reformer who fights alone or the political patriot who fights under the cover of vast mass of supporters?[18]

Ambedkar was in favour of social reformation. He had observed that,

> no one can say that to have the problems of social reform put aside is a desirable state of things whenever there are social evils. The health of body politic requires that they shall be removed before they become the symbols of suffering and injustice. For it is the social and economic evil which everywhere are the parent of revolution or decay.[19]

This approach of Ambedkar clearly reveals his vision of social justice. He thus wanted to bring a new change in Indian society. In such new order he believed that, the country needs a lead and the question is, who can give this lead?

I venture to say that labour is capable of giving to the country the lead it needs. Correct leadership apart from other things requires idealism and free thoughts.[20]

Ambedkar believed that, "social reforms are more fundamental than political reforms."[21]

Thus we have to understand the socio-legal philosophy of Ambedkar. According to Harris, "the legal theory is used to cover inquiries into the nature of law."[22]

---

18. Ibid.
19. Ibid.
20. Ibid., p. 19
21. Ibid., p. 20
22. J.W. Harris, *Legal Philosophies*, London: Butterworth, 1983, p. 5.

In order to theorize on the legal philosophy of Ambedkar we have to study his contribution to the field of social justice. He firmly believed in liberty, equality and social justice and freedom. According to Bertrand Russell,

> freedom covers only those who no longer ask of life that it shall yield them any of those personal goods that are subject to the mutation of time.[23]

It is true that freedom must be used for good and right cause of the development of individuals as well as community as a whole. Ambedkar was highly influenced by Western liberal values. According to Prof. V.N. Gajendragadkar,

> the social progressive values that Dr Ambedkar cherished were the basis of his social and political life.[24]

Though he was born in the Mahar community, he never represented his own community but represented all those communities which were socially and economically down-trodden. Ambedkar thus became a champion of social justice to all weaker sections in the community. Hence his ideas are related to all the weaker sections in the developing countries. The study of philosophy of law is related to the welfare of the people.

It was rightly pointed out by Ambedkar that,

> law and public opinion are forces which govern the conduct of man. They act and react upon each other.[25]

Further while interpreting the difference between law and public opinion Ambedkar had pointed out that,

---

23. Amita Singh, *The Political Philosophy of Betrand Russell* 1987, p. 71.
24. V.N. Gajendragadkar, "Minority and Backward Community," in *Ambedkar and Social Justice*, Publications Division, GOI, 1992, p. 296.
25. N.G. Kamble, K.M. Kamble, M.L. Kasane op. cit., p. 104.

> at times law goes ahead of public opinion and checks it and redirects it in channels which it thinks proper; at times public opinion is ahead of the Law.[26]

We have to highlight Ambedkar's views in the context of social welfare. About responsibilities of modern welfare state in social justice, he had pointed out that,

> to protect itself against external aggression, maintain law and order against internal disturbance and guarantee to its subject minimum standards of administration and welfare, which are expected from a modern state.[27]

He had further noted that,

> if democracy is to live up to its principle of one man, one value, law of the constitution should not only prescribe the shape and form of the political structure but also must prescribe the shape and form of the economic structure of society.[28]

His ideas were based on liberty, equality, fraternity and social justice. He had stated that,

> in vast aspects of social life, people are left free to carry on without interference of law, or if law has to be made, then the law maker expect that society will have enough morality in it to make a law a success.[29]

Ambedkar had longer vision of developing Indian society on the basis of morality and rule of law. The whole purpose of his sociological philosophy was to develop Indian democracy in a mature way. He wanted to establish democracy in India

---

26. Ibid.
27. Ibid., p. 105.
28. Ibid. p. 106.
29. Ibid.,

as a way of life. Yogendra Maqwana had rightly analysed about the future of democracy. He had observed that,

> the main object of Ambedkar's life was to bring social revolution. He wanted to break the system of *varnas* and caste so that everybody gets the opportunity of self-development. For this he adopted democratic and constitutional means. This was therefore dominated by constitutional and democratic ideologies. He wanted to transform political democracy into social democracy.[30]

On this background it would be interesting to study the social philosophy of Ambedkar.

A brief historical background of development of social philosophy can be presented here.

Article 25 of the Indian Constitution refers to throwing open of Hindu temples to all sections of Hindus. In this connection, Article 252(b) is referred to as, "providing for social welfare and reform or the throwing open of Hindu religions institutions of a public character to all classes and sections of Hindus."[31]

The Supreme Court has tried to provide a new approach to the problem of reservation especially the recent decision of Supreme Court, in the matter of *Ajit Singh* v. *State of Punjab and others*.

The Supreme Court has tried to balance the conflicting interest amongst employees belonging to the open category on one hand and Reserved category on the other hand. The Supreme Court, in its decision pointed out that,

> it is so heartening to note that those for whom the founding

30. S.S. Sashi, "Collected Works of Dr Ambedkar" in *Ambedkar and Social Justice*, vol. I, Publications Division, GOI, 1992, p. 68.

31. V.N. Shukla, *Constitution of India*, 7th edn., 1988, pp. 142-43.

> fathers introduced the provision for reservation to protect and encourage entry in service, now are able to enter service on their own merit by competing with candidates of general category. For promotion or appointment of a member of Scheduled Castes against the post reserved for him, the primary question to be considered is as to whether he belongs to a class for whom reservation has been made. But for consideration for appointment or promotion against a general category post, merit is the primary consideration because the applicant is to enter into the service or grade of service through merit channel.[32]

Further the decision has highlighted that,

> when framers of the Constitution by Article 16 guaranteed equality of opportunity in matters of public employment, they aimed at combining democratization with efficiency. In the process of democratization Article 16(4) enabled the State to make provisions for reservation of appointments or posts in favour of any backward class of citizens, which in the opinion of the State is not adequately represented in the services under the State.

Broadly speaking the legal point of view behind its decision was that,

> all concerned who are involved and interested in the upliftment and growth of the nation have to work out a system by which the injustice done to a section of people in our society at certain period of history can be rectified by providing protections to their descendants. But we have to be conscious at the same time that the efficiency of the administration of the country is not harmed and there is no reverse discrimination.[33]

---

32. *Ajit Singh Januja & others* vs *State of Panjab A.I.R.* 1996, S.C., p. 1199.

33. Ibid., p. 1200 (para 15).

This was in tune with the principles of social democracy championed by Ambedkar. The decision further explained the principle of equality in the new context and had noted that

> the equality principle requires exclusion of the factor of extra-weightage of earlier promotion to a reserved category candidate because of reservation alone when he competes for further promotion to a general category with a general category candidate senior to him in the panel. Any other view would amount to reverse discrimination and violative of the guarantee of equality in Articles 14 to 16.

Thus Ambedkar's vision and philosophy of social justice has been reinterpreted by Hon'ble Supreme Court in a relevant manner.

1

Social Realities in the Pre-Buddhist Era

DRINKING was another evil which was rampant among the Indo-Aryans. The liquor (*soma*) was in the beginning permitted only to the *traivarnikas*. Subsequently, it was permitted only to the first two castes. But *sura* was opened to all. Shukracharya, the priest drank so heavily that in his drunken state he gave the life-giving *mantra* (*mritasanjivani mantra*), known to him only and with which he used to revive the *asuras* killed by the *devas*, to Kacha, the son of Brihaspati.

The best among the Indo-Aryans were also addicted to drinking. The most shameful part of it was that even the Indo-Aryan women were free for drinking. There were various instances in which women were addicted to liquor. Sudeshna (*Mahabharata*,Vanaparva, XV.10) — the wife of King Virat — tells her maid Sairandhri to go to Kichaka's palace and bring *sura* as she was dying to have a drink. Brahmin women as well as women of all classes were not free from such habit during the pre-Buddhist period. "Four or eight women who are not widowed after having been regaled with wine and food are to dance for times in the night previous to the wedding ceremony." *Kausitaki Grihya-Sutra* II.11-12 and Kumarila Bhatta (*Tantravartika* I.iii.4) Condemned such practice among the women.[1]

1. *Kausitaki Grihya-Sutra* II.11.12 and Kumarila Bhatta (*Tantravarttika* I.iii.4).

Sexual immorality of the Indo-Aryan society must shock their present-day descendants. The Indo-Aryans of the pre-Buddhist days had no such rule of prohibition to govern their sexual or matrimonial relationship. According to the Indo-Aryan mythology, Brahma had three sons and a daughter. One of the sons Daksha married his sister. The daughters born of this marriage between brother and sister were married to Kashyapa, the son of Marich, the son of Brahma (*Mahabharata*, Adiparva, 66).[2]

Yami, the sister of Yama, was stated to have invited her brother Yama to cohabit with her and became angry when he refused to yield to her. Rigveda married his own daughter Shatarupa when she came of age (*Harivansha*, X).[3] Jahnu married his daughter Jahnavi (*Harivansha*, XXVII)[4] and Surya married his daughter Usha (Yaska *Nirukta*, V).[5]

Polyandry was prevalent in the Indo-Aryan society. Dhahaprachetani and his son Soma cohabited with Marisha, the daughter of Soma (*Harivansha*, II). Daksha gave his daughter in marriage to his father Brahma and from that marriage was born Narada (*Harivansha*, III).[6] Dauhitra gave his twenty-seven daughters to his father Soma for procreation (*Harivansha*, III).[7]

There were instances of immoral practices of the great *rishis* in the name of religious rites. Parashara had sexual intercourse with Satyavati and also Dirghatapa. The King Yayati gave his daughter Madhavi as on offering to his Guru

2. *Mahabharata*, Adiparva, p. 66.
3. *Harivansha* (X).
4. Ibid., XXVII.
5. Yaska *Nirukta* V.
6. *Harivansha*, III.
7. Ibid., III., p. 155.

Galava. Galava rented out the girl Madhavi to three kings each for a period. Thereafter, he gave her in marriage to Vishvamitra. She remained with him until a son was born to her. Thereafter, Galava took away the girl and gave her back to her father Yayati.[8]

In the Indo-Aryan society, there was no rule of chastity for maidens. A girl could have intercourse with and also progeny from anybody without contracting marriage. Kunti had children from different men before she was married to Pandu. Matsyaganti had sexual intercourse with the sage Parashara before she was married to Shantanu. Bestiality was also prevalent in the Indo-Aryan society. The most hideous instance was that of the women having sexual intercourse with the horse in the *Ashvamedha yajna*. Women had more than one husband and man had many number of wives.

The priestly profession of the ancient Indo-Aryan society was the monopoly of the brahmins. Such a profession was supposed to have been a holy one and the priests were supposed to be guides of the people in the moral and spiritual matters and they were to set the standard for people to follow. But, really, the brahmin priests led lives of luxury and were anti-religious. They had fallen to the utmost depth of moral degradation.

The brahmins were addicted to visiting shows such as *nautch dance*, fair sites, etc., games, recreations, to the use of high and large couches and to the use of means for adorning and beautifying themselves. They were also addicted to such low conversations such as gossips at street corners, tales about women, etc. and to the use of wrangling phrases, to the taking of messages, going on errands and acting as go-betweens.

---

8. Ibid., III., p. 156.

The brahmins earned their livelihood by wrong means such as palmistry, snake charming, etc.

Just as sexual relation among the Indo-Aryans was of a loose sort, the system of their diet was also very vulgar. They were not only meat-eaters but also beef-eaters. From the brahmins to the shudras everybody ate meat. Such a social system existed in Bharata round about 500 BCE.

Even Gods had supported the venomous system of caste. It is evident from the Puranas: "I myself have created the arrangement known as *chaturvarna*" (*Bhagavad Gita,* IV.13), i.e. the division of society into four castes. According to Hopkins the period of *Bhagavad-Gita* is roughly calculated to be between CE 200 and 400. Even though the Mahabharata war between the Kauravas and Pandavas was a very ancient event, that does not mean that the composition of Vyas was as old as the event or contemporaneous with the event. The *Mahabharata* had different editions at different times. Subsequent editions have been made in later times or the various recastings in verbal form, which may safely be assumed to have occurred at the hands of successive copyists. Even at the end of twentieth century, the Indian epics have been recomposed to suit television telecasting by episodes having entirely different versions than those of the old epics.

Advent of Buddhism

As already detailed, the Indo-Aryan society was in a wretched condition which required immediate purification. To subside all these evils there was the intense necessity of social, cultural and political reform in the Indo-Aryan society. Gautama Buddha was the first social revolutionary reformer to reform the Indo-Aryan Society, History of social reform in Bharata began with Gautama.

Siddhartha *alias* Gautama was born in 563 BCE at Kapilavastu in north India on the borders of Nepal. The historians often claimed Siddhartha to be prince of the Indo-Aryan community but their claim is contrary to historical truth. His father was the chief of a tribal community who was subjected to great ignominies at the hands of the Indo-Aryan brahmins. His community was destined to suffer tyranny and frustration because of caste distinction and discrimination.

On keen observation of his life, it can be judged that Gautama was not a kshatriya by caste but he belonged to a downtrodden community which was striving hard for liberation from the yoke of Brahmanical social order. Historical evidences are numerous in support of the argument that he was not of a *chaturvarna* group.

The study of the history of the world reveals that no man, who has not suffered at the hands of such oppressive social order, ever revolted against the existing social order. Gautama revolted against the social evil that his community was subjected to. It is a bare truth of history that those who live in luxury, comfort and free from troubles and miseries, have never dared or tried to console the poor and liberate them from the yoke of their serfdom. World famous revolutionaries such as Christ, Nabi, Abraham Lincoln, Marx, Ambedkar, Ayyankali, etc. were great examples. No exception to this rule or theory can be traced out from the history of the world.

Revolution is the echo of bitter suffering. Oppressed by the evils, misery, misfortune and sufferings, Gautama led the revolution against Brahmanism and caste system. For those who had no experience in life, it is unnatural that they can have a burning and revolutionary mind. (E.M. Sankaran Namboodiripad was a communist even though he was born in brahmin community which upheld the philosophy of Manu. But when he found that the women of his community also were oppressed by their own social philosophy itself, he voiced against such evils and became a revolutionary.[9])

It was by dint of hard thinking and solitary meditation that Gautama got insight into things and as a result of his insight Gautama became enlightened and formalized his own *dhamma (dharma* in Sanskrit).

Gautama attained enlightenment at the age of thirty-five. Because of his insight, he was called the Buddha. Buddha means one who got insight. For eighty years, he spent his time in spreading his *dhamma* and founding and administering an order of monks, i.e. devoted volunteers.

The Buddha was more advanced in the subtle points of inner development directing the affairs of the order of discipline, confirming the faithful in their virtue deputations carrying on discussions with learned opponents, comforting the sorrowful, and visiting kings and peasants, brahmins and out-castes, rich and poor.[10]

The cause for the rapid spread of Buddhism in a country where the vulgar Indo-Aryan society existed was explained by Hopkins thus:

> No man ever lived so godless yet so godlike, arrogating to himself no divinity, despairing of future bliss, but without fear as without hope, leader of thought but adored, the universal brother, he wandered among men simply serenly, with gentle irony subduing them that opposed him, congregation after congregation, speaking with majestic sweetness, the master to each, the friend of all.[11]

The Buddha laboured to reform the Indo-Aryan society by applying new methods and new thinking entirely different

9. B.R. Ambedkar, *Writings and Speeches*, II, p. 166.
10. Ibid., III, p. 167.
11. H.P. Ghentharassory, op. cit., p. 56.

from that of the existing one. He had given some guidelines: *buddham sharanam, dhammam sharanam, sangham sharanam.*

The philosophy of the Buddha can be placed in a nutshell that,

> craving is the cause of grasping, craving gives rise to pursuit of gain. If there was no pursuit of gain, there would not arise passion. If there was no passion, tenacity would not arise. If there would not be love for private possession there would be peace. By extirpating all cravings by not lusting after them, but by destroying and abandoning and renouncing them all, one could acquire enlightenment.

The teaching of Buddha swept the land as no physical conqueror had ever done in Indian history. Within a few generations almost the entire country especially the suffering masses and the trading classes went over to Buddhism. It soon became the religion of the whole of India. Religion is not in the spiritual sense. It was only a way of living a virtuous, pure and worthy life upholding the way of non-violence. It did not remain confined to India alone. It reached every nook and corner of the then known world. Though it was started as a religious revolution overshadowing the Indo-Aryans' philosophy or customs it was more than a religious revolution. It took the shape of a social as well as political revolution. It ended as a solution for casteism and other exploitations.[12]

Buddhism spread a new moral code such as: not to kill, not to steal, not to lie, not to be unchaste, and not to drink intoxicants. Such a moral life it preached was quite unknown to the Indo-Aryan society. It repudiated the authority of the Vedas and denounced the practice of sacrifice. Its ideals were contrary to that of Brahmanism. It denounced graded inequality and accepted all people to the rank of equals and offered equality of opportunity to all. In short, Buddhism was

12. Dhananjay Keer, *Life and Mission*, p. 275.

anti-Brahmanism in all respects, i.e. Buddhism was the negative of Brahmanism.

Bindusara, the son of Chandragupta, assumed the imperial throne in 298 BCE. His son Ashoka was enthroned as king in 273 BCE. Details about his religion are available from the edicts of Ashokan pillars, the inscriptions on which were the oldest of Indian inscriptions hitherto deciphered. He was a staunch follower of the Buddha and devoted his whole life after the Kalinga war for the propagation of Buddhism in India as well as abroad.

Ashoka made Buddhism the religion of the state. This was, of course, the greatest blow to Brahmanism. Brahmanism lost all state patronage and were neglected to a secondary and subsidiary position in the empire of Ashoka. In effect, Brahmanism became suppressed for the simple reason that Ashoka prohibited animal sacrifices which constituted the very essence of Brahmanic religion. Brahmanism had not only lost state patronage, but also the brahmins lost their occupation which mainly consisted in performing sacrifice for a fee which often was very substantial and which constituted their chief source of living. The brahmins, therefore, lived as a suppressed and depressed class for nearly one hundred and forty years during which the Mauryan Empire lasted (the inferiority complex of the brahmins under the Mauryan rule becomes apparent from the privileges asked for them by Manu in the *Manusmriti*. The inferiority complex must be due to their depressed condition. They kept up their vengeance towards the shudras (adi-shudras) which led to the constitution of *Manusmriti*. The anti-Dalit attitude of the present day casteists is mainly due to their age-old vengeance towards the adi-shudras namely the followers of Jainism and Buddhism.

After Ashoka, due to internal struggles the Mauryan Empire began to decline. So was the fate of Buddhism. As

Buddhism was the whirlwind of revolution against Brahmanism, it paved the way for the formation of society devoid of caste and inequality. Not only the dialectical nature of the Buddhist society led to its decline but also the staunch enmity of Brahmanism and their united struggles for the re-establishment of Brahmanism were the other causes. It was after two hundred and eighteen years after the demise of the Buddha that the Third Buddhist Council was held, i.e. in 246 BCE. The main purpose of the Council was to expel the enemies who in disguise of supporters and sympathisers infiltrated into the gang of Buddhism to sabotage it. The conference recommended the ruler, Ashoka to expel the sixty thousand brahmin spies from Buddhism and also re-examine the Pan laws.

The decision of the Buddhist Council provoked the Indo-Aryans as a result of which numerous collisions occurred throughout the country. Certain rulers who pretended to be tolerant towards Buddhism and at the same time in the heart of heart supported Brahmanism (just as the twentieth- century Indian politics) sent numerous Buddhist saints to the gallows. In most places, the Buddhists lost freedom of religious works. After the times of Ashoka, not only the influence and power of Brahmanism increased but disquietude and violence also increased. The last Mauryan rulers who gave help and support to the Buddhists were inefficient to resist the Indo-Aryan group rivalry, and internal struggles began to rise among the Buddhists when they lost the support of the rulers.

There were also various other factors which led to the decline of Buddhism. The rulers as well as a majority of the wealthy classes had rushed into this religion with bad intentions. They wanted to dominate it thereby catching hold of leadership. In the beginning, Buddhism got some publicity through the influence of the newcomers (recall the history of the political parties in India which came forward in the name of the labouring classes) but the net result was adverse growth.

Whenever the enemies come forward with helping hands, their motive behind it should be analysed well. They can use the destructive weapon wherever chances await them. This had happened in the case of Jainism and Buddhism. This had happened in modern times in the case of Marxism also.

The successors of Ashoka were inefficient as rulers. Half a dozen Mauryan kings had ruled after Ashoka, concurrently over several parts of his empire. Ashoka's grandson Dasharatha (not of the *Ramayana*) presented the Barabar cave to the Ajivikas while a successor Samprati is supported its prestige long after royal power had vanished. The last descendant of Ashoka, Purnavarman of Magadha, restored the *bodhi* tree and Buddhist foundation at Gaya after Shashanka's destructive raid.

A Barbarian risen to power by name Kharavela raided deep into the heartland from Kalinga reversing Ashoka's victory.

The regicide and the Brahmanic revolution (details in the next chapter) disturbed the society of that time. Patanjali's grammar and Sanskrit prose also belong to the time of Pushyamitra Shunga. The Shungas retained their hereditary title of Sonnai after mounting the throne. Kalidasa's *Malavikagnimitram* deals centuries later with the love story of Pushyamitra's son, a victory at Ujjain. The Brahmanical rule of the Shungas ended with the last Shunga who was assassinated by his brahmin minister Kavayana to usurp the throne.

The Satavahana's origin was with a brahmin husband and a Naga wife. Prakrit literature developed its first output under the Satavahanas whose rule faded away in the third century CE.

The great Buddhist centres at Nagarjunakonda on the southern bank of the River Krishna, and at Kanchi were founded before the second century CE. Between the Satavahanas and the Guptas (fourth century CE) lies an interlude of small invasions and aboriginal chief trying to capture the kingship. Among these, last, were several Nagas of the Gangetic plains.

Chandragupta I (CE 320-35) who married Kumaradevi of Licchavi had a hold over Kosala and part of Magadha. The final conquest came under his son Samudragupta (CE 335-75). Chandragupta II styled as Vikramaditya (CE 379-414) married Naga princess Kubera Naga. Fahian visited India at this time. Chandragupta II extended his country into Assam, Afghanistan, towards Central Asia and up to Deccan.

In the period after Christ, the people who were called shudras or nagas (the *varna bahyas*) became the founders of the excellent culture and civilization. They had matrimonial alliance with the foremost royal families in India. Not only they had excellent culture, but also had sovereignty in different parts of India. Their prominent centre of inhabitation was Maharashtra. In the beginning of Christain era, they had sway over India and in the neighbouring states. The Satavahanas ruled Andhra with capital at Srikakula. They had invaded and annexed Malwa, Hyderabad, and Maharashtra.

During this period brahmins were in a captive condition. They could not raise their heads. During the dominance of the Satavahanas, Buddhism flourished in its heights. The Buddhist monuments at Sanchi in Madhya Pradesh, Amaravati Pillars in Andhra Pradesh, Taxila at Peshawar (Pakistan), Sarnath at Varanasi and the hundreds of Buddhist *viharas* were built at the time of Satavahanas. The multitude of *viharas* built at a certain state furnished it with the beautiful name Bihar.

The people who belonged to the Naga clan had used the word "Naga" with their names.

During the third and fourth centuries the Nagas were in power in most of the counties throughout India. There were numerous evidences to show that the Nagas ruled Saurashtra till sixth century CE. The people who were called Nagas or Dravidians ruled not only in south India but also in different parts of north India. Their power extended from Taxila in north-west India to the north-eastern Assam and also in Ceylon. These Nagas who were interested in sailing merged with the Cheras also. These people from ancient times were called Chera (Sera), Chola or Pandyan in the south. They were in another name in the Puranas as Assura. The Dravidians of the south India and the Nagas or Assuras of north India were the same people. Kanauj, Haiva, Gandhara, Bhoda, Sudesa, Kuntala, Nepal, Sahujavatika, Kekaya, Pandia, etc. were their dominant centres.

Influence of Buddhism on Indian History

Buddhism was a way of ideal and good life aiming at leading a pure and virtuous life so that it might serve as a model to all. It aimed at moulding the character of the ordinary man and woman in the society. It devised a form of baptism for observing certain moral precepts. This was the highest standard for a moral life for an individual to follow. In fact, high standard of moral life was quite unknown to the Indo-Aryan society. Such was the high quality of the philosophy of the Buddha that Brahmanism dared in course of time to claim that the philosophy of Buddhism has close relation and similarity to that of Hinduism. Certain philosophers of Hinduism were not shy to claim that Buddhism was another developed form of Hinduism and Buddha himself was an incarnation of Vishnu. His name was included in the later years in the list of incarnation of Vishnu as ninth *avatara*. These were utter follies. This was another deception by the brahmin scholars because Buddhism is quite opposite to the principles of Brahmanism.

There was a side-effect of the revolution of Buddhism. Brahmanism was to a certain extent refined by the teachings of the Buddha. Even the teaching of Kaladi Shankaracharya were to a certain extent influenced by the philosophy of the Buddha. The teachings of Buddhism which were very much appealing to the masses were his gospel of social equality, his demand for abolition of the system of *chaturvarna*, his doctrine of non-violence and his condemnation of elaborate religious ceremonials and sacrifices which impoverished the masses and created among them a repugnance for religious ceremonies. Brahmanism of the period of the Buddha sacrificed cows and other animals in thousands, presumably to pacify the gods but really to pacify the priests' own greed for meat.

The brahmins' demand for meat on such an unbounded scale impoverished the peasants who had to find the cows for the sacrifices and consequently had been deprived of milk and its by-products which were their staple means of livelihood.

By the influence of the teachings of the Buddha, the brahmins became strict vegetarians; wine bibbling came to an end; Brahmanism assumed a puritanical covering. In order to prevent the kshatriyas going over to Buddhism, Brahmanism offered them equality with themselves.

Cow being sanctified, sacrificial ceremonials were brought to an end and a large number of other Buddhist teachings were incorporated in Brahmanism. The masses who had gone over to Buddhism have slowly begun to leave it.

The one great teaching that the brahmins could accept was the theory of equality and the abolition of *chaturvarna* caste system. But they did one thing for the time being — they relegated the gods in their places and came to other time serving compromises.

Brahmanism gradually stopped cow killing and sacrifices as advised by Buddha. Animals were sanctified by the Brahmanism. The brahmin society in general accepted the sanctification and stopped killing of cows. Neither the Buddhists nor the brahmins had forbidden consumption of carcases. Ban was only against slaughtering of live cows. One of the later developments of the ideal of *chaturvarna* is the creation of the fifth *varna* next below the shudras and the other is the separation of the shudras from the first three *varna*s.

These changes have become so integrated with the original scheme of the *Purusha-Sukta* that they have given rise to peculiar terms and expressions so well known that everybody understands what they stand for.

These terms are: *savarna, avarna, dvija, and traivarnika*. They stand to indicate the sub-divisions of the original four classes and the degree of separation between them.

The untouchables or the adi-shudras are outside the four walls of the *varna* system, i.e. they are a casteless people.

Dvija is generally contrasted with non-*dvija*. *Dvija* literally means twice-born and non-*dvija* means one who is born only once. The distinction is based on the right to have *Upanayana* which is treated as second birth. Those who have the right to wear the sacred thread or panel are called *dvija*.

Shudras and adi-shudras have no right to wear the sacred thread. Both are non-*dvija*s but as a major part of the shudras who supported and obeyed the provisions of *Manusmriti*, sided with the *dvija*s but not mingled with the *savarna*s. At the same time, those shudras who vehemently protested and rebelled against *Manusmriti* were ousted from the fourth *varna* and categorized under *avarna* group, i.e. casteless group. Those who are outcastes or *avarnas* were treated as enemies of the *chaturvarnikas* and so many restrictions were imposed on them which had no parallel anywhere in the world.

The Origin of Caste

Manu is considered as the progenitor of caste but he is not responsible for the creation of caste. The statement in the *Mahabharata* that caste system or *Chaturvarnya* is the creation of Lord Krishna, is historically unfounded. Caste system is the creation of man and not God. In *Rigveda*, there is a reference to the *varna* system but not caste system. It is a reference to the class of people. Manu preached the sanctity of *varna*. *Varna* is only the parent of caste. In that sense, Manu can be charged with being the progenitor if not the author of caste system.

In the scheme of Manu, the brahmin is placed at the first rank. Below him is the kshatriya. Below the kshatriya is the vaishya and below it is the shudra. These four groups formed the caste people. Those who were bitterly against these groups were casteless and they were treated as the fifth group outside the caste system and they are called adi-shudras or the indigenous Indians. In course of time, the indigenous people were treated as untouchables. This system of rank and gradation is simply another way of enforcing the principle of inequality so that it may be truly said that Hinduism does not recognize equality. In the absence of equality, there cannot be brotherhood. It is a permanent social relationship among the classes to be observed and enforced at all time in all places and for all purposes.

The Hindu society was originally divided into four *varnas*

or classes. The *varna* was based on worth but as time went on the *varna* came to be based on birth and thus, the four *varnas* came to be known as four castes. According to Ambedkar, the caste system is a social division of people of the same race and is not merely a division of labour but also a division of labourers — compelling a man to engage himself in a calling which may not appeal to him. The *varna* system has a tendency to degenerate into a caste system. The caste system dreadens, paralyses and cripples the people from helpful activity. Now, is the caste system eugenic in origin? It is a social system which embodies the arrogance and selfishness of a perverse section of the Hindus who were superior enough in social status to set it in fashion and who had the authority to force it on the inferiors.

Caste is the bane of the Hindus. It is the cause of the downfall of the Hindus. Caste had made the Hindus the sickmen of India. Caste has ruined the Hindu race and has destroyed, demoralized and devitalized humanity.

The fusion of blood alone can create a feeling of being kith and kin. Caste is a notion, a state of mind. Its distinction means a notional change. Hindus observe caste not because they are inhuman and wrong-headed but because they are deeply religious. Their religion inculcates this notion of caste. The real enemy is the Shastras (scriptures) which teach them this religion of caste. Destroy this belief in the sanctity of such Shastras. Destroy the authority, the sacredness and divinity of such Shastras and the Vedas which preach partiality among human beings. Ambedkar urged for making every man and woman free from the thralldom to such Shastras and he or she will intermarry.

The main feature of Indian society seen at its strongest in the rural countryside is caste. This means the division of society into many groups which live side by side, but often do not seem to live together as members of different castes not inter-married by religion in spite of the permission by law. Most peasants will not take cooked food or drink water from the hands of lower caste persons. The number of such caste groups goes into thousands. In theory, there were only four castes. Of the four castes, shudra is considered to be the lowest which corresponds in general to the working class. The relative status of the local castes depends always upon the extent of, and the caste's economic position in the common market.

The lower a caste goes in the economic scale, the lower is the caste in the social scale on the whole. At the lowest end of the caste are tribal-groups many of whom are in the food gathering stage. The surrounding general society is now food producing. So, these very low castes eked out livelihood generally by begging and stealing. Such nether-most groups were labelled the "criminal tribes" by the British; they refused to acknowledge law and order outside the tribes.

This stratification of Indian society reflects and explains in general a great deal of Indian history. The legends and religious observations were rewritten by the brahmins to suit themselves and to give brahmin caste predominance in the priesthood, which in the lower castes is generally not in the hands of brahmins. The Hindu culture and the literate traditions often go back to much older times. The main work of the brahmins has been to gather the myths together to display them as unified cycles of stories and to set them in a better developed social framework. Indian society seemed to develop more by successive religious transformation than by violence. Most of the surviving ancient Indian documents are overwhelmingly religious and ritualistic. Trying to extract history from them without some previous knowledge of actual structure of Indian society at the time of writing gives either no result or the ludicrous conclusions that may be read in most of the histories of India.

The brahmins who are claimed to be the natural leaders of the Hindus and form the intellectual class will not lead the movement to destroy the power and the prestige of the priests. So, Ambedkar suggests the distinction of the idea of hereditary priesthood and democratization of the profession of priests by the grant of a *sanad* to any Hindu who passes a certain test and by narrowing down the number of priests. Ambedkar proposes to kill this Brahmanism to save Hinduism. Hindu should have one common religious book. Hindu society needs moral regeneration and it is dangerous to postpone it. It is what history calls for. Only when Hindu society becomes a casteless society that it can hope to have strength enough to defend itself.

Ambedkar's call for reorganization of the Hindu society is a continuation of preachings of the modern leaders such as Swami Shraddhananda, Lala Lajpat Rai, Raja Rammohun Roy, Bhai Paramanand, Acharya P.C. Roy, R.C. Dutt, Bipin Chandra Pal, Aurobindo Ghosh, Ramananda Chatterji, Lala Har Dayal, St. Kabir, Chaitanya, St. Ekanath, St. Tukaram, St. Ravidas, St. Chokhamela, Mahatma Phule, Ranade, Narayana Guru, Ayyankali, and a host of others having a long chain of social reformers down from the Buddha.

History of India holds that the caste system among the Hindus has deprived the Hindus of strong nationalistic, patriotic, and solidarity feelings. Caste grows by fusion; it is antagonistic to national union. As caste being the curse of India, it in all its forms has made India a nation of slaves. No foreign religion or foreign power has destroyed the integrity and greatness of India as has been done by Brahmanism. Our enemy is within India. Priest craft and caste have slain us.

India can never establish and maintain a free state so long as there are caste rules in our society. Caste-Hindus can never work together or establish a free state or create victorious army as long as casteism dominates India.

In short, caste system, which is the backbone of Brahmanism is the bane of Hinduism, is the verdict given by India's great and true historians and sociologists, leaders of thought and social reformers. That the upholders of the Brahmanical social order pride themselves on caste feelings is not far from truth. Ninety per cent of the atrocities, cruelties, and other religion based crimes in India are the result of the caste feeling. The political parties inspired by Brahmanism are instigating disharmony and enmity among the various communities. They encourage terrorism and violence.

Attitude of Casteists towards Spread of Education

In the matter of spread of education, two conditions are prerequisites. There must be formal education. There must be literacy. Without these two, knowledge cannot be spread. Without formal education it is not possible to transmit all the resources and achievements of a complex society. Without formal education, the accumulated thoughts and experiences relating to a subject cannot be passed on to the younger generation and they will never get it if they were left to pick up their training in informal association with others. Without formal education, they will not get new perceptions. Their horizon will not be widened and they will remain as ignorant slave of their routine work. But formal education involves the establishment of special agencies such as schools, books, planned materials such as studies, etc. How can anyone take advantage of these special agencies of formal education unless he is literate and able to read and write? The spread of the art of reading and writing, i.e. literacy and formal education go hand in hand; without the existence of the two, there can be no spread of knowledge.

The concept of formal education in Hinduism was of a very limited character. Formal education was confined only to the study of the Vedas for the Hindus believed that there was no knowledge outside the Vedas. That being so, formal education was confined to the study of the Vedas and the consequence was that the Hindu recognized that his only duty was to study in the schools established for the study of the Vedas. These schools benefited only the brahmins. The state did not take responsibility for opening centres for the study of arts and sciences which concerned the life of the merchants and the artisans.

In ancient days education was domestic. It only increased the skill to do a particular thing. It did not lead to new perception. It did not widen the horizon with the result that the practical education taught to him was only an isolated and uniform way of acting. Illiteracy became an inherent part of Brahmanism. To foster illiteracy and ignorance among the mass, Manu formed rules saying brahmins alone have the right to teach the Vedas. But in the case of shudras, he is not only prohibited to study the Vedas, he should not also be allowed to hear or to read it. The study of the Vedas was made an offence to shudras. In the words of Gautama (XII-4), if the shudra intentionally listen for committing to memory the Vedas then his ears should be filled with (molten) lead and lac; if he has mastered the Vedas, his body should be cut into pieces.

Manu has denied the common man the right to knowledge. The prohibition against the study of the Vedas to masses of the people gave rise to illiteracy and ignorance.

Brahmins were the authors of the whole body of the Hindu religious literature except the Upanishad (Literature). They were very particular and careful to inject the doctrine formulated by them in the Smritis, Vedas and the *Gita*. The philosophy of brahmins will be the same whether one takes Smritis as its gospel or whether one takes Vedas and the *Gita* as the gospel of Hinduism.

Two Kinds of Human Beings in the Land of Gods and Goddesses

Caste has been a growing institution. It has never been the same at all time. The shape and form of caste as it existed when Magasthanese (305 BCE) wrote his account of the social condition in Bharata, was very different from what form and shape it had taken when Alberuni (CE 1030) came. The way it appeared to the Portuguese (CE 1500) was different from what it was during the time of Alberuni.

The four classes (*varna*s) were for a time merely classes. After a time what were only classes (*varna*s) became castes (*jati*s) and the four castes became four thousand. In this way, the modern caste system was only the evolution of the ancient *varna* system.

A Hindu is born in a caste and he dies as a member of that caste. There is no Hindu without a caste. None can escape caste and being bound by caste from birth to death, he becomes subject to social regulations and traditions of the caste over which he has no control.

Caste is a perversion of *varna*, and at any rate is an evolution in the opposite direction. But, while caste has completely perverted the *varna* system, it has borrowed the class system from the *varna* system.

In India, castes are not merely non-social. Often they are anti-social. This is particularly true of the Hindus towards the untouchables. This can be proved when the attitude of the caste-Hindus is subjected to study. For instance, the Hindus did not allow the downtrodden to take water from a common well. The caste-Hindu hesitated to allow the casteless to wear jewellery. They were forbidden from using tiles for their houses. The caste-Hindus were least interested in tolerating the outcastes to own land, cattle and other wealth. They were not allowed any human rights. They are the emanations of the permanent antisocial attitude of the caste-Hindus against the casteless.

There have been many reformers, who long before M.K. Gandhi came on the scene, tried to remove the strain of untouchability. But they all failed. The reason for their failure is that they have nothing to fear from the untouchables, nor have they anything to gain by the abolition of untouchability. The caste-Hindus once at the time of emergence of Buddhism gave up beef eating because they were afraid that otherwise Buddhism would overpower Hinduism.

The brahmins of Akbar's time wrote *Allah-Upanishad* to give a place of Akbar's *Din-i-Ilahi* within Hinduism and to recognize it as the seventh system of Hindu philosophy. It means that Hinduism can absorb many things. The beef eating Hinduism *alias* Brahmanism absorbed the non-violence theory of Buddhism and became a religion of vegetarianism but did not care to abolish untouchability or caste system. Brahmanism wrote *Allah-Upanishad* because they had everything to gain by helping Akbar to establish a new religion. They gained money by pleasing the emperor and by lending aid to establish a religion which promised less tyranny and oppression to the Hindus than Islam held out. Neither of these considerations exist for the most sanguine among the outcastes to expect that the Hindu will readily put an end to this curse of untouchability.

Not only have the caste-Hindus nothing to fear and nothing to gain; they have, in fact, much to lose by the abolition of untouchability.

The system of untouchability is a gold mine to the Hindus. In it they have good population of the untouchables to serve as their retinue to enable the Hindus to maintain pomp and ceremony and to cultivate a feeling of pride and dignity befitting a master class which cannot be fostered and sustained unless there is beneath it a servile class to look down upon. In it the Hindus have the outcastes to be used as forced labour and because of their state of complete destitution and helplessness can be compelled to work on a mere pittance and sometimes on nothing at all.

The caste-Hindus have the outcastes to do the daily work of scavengers and sweepers which the caste-Hindus were debarred by his religion to do and which must be done for the Hindus by non-Hindus who could be none other than the outcastes.

It is these outcastes who can be kept to do lower jobs and prevented from entering into competition from higher jobs preserved for the Hindus. It is the millions of outcastes who can be used as shock absorbers in slums and dead-weight in booms, for the caste-Hindus are fired last and in booms the Hindu is employed first and the outcaste is employed last.

Untouchability — the Leprosy of Hinduism

Untouchability is an attitude of the Hindus. For untouchability to vanish, it is the Hindu who must change. History will not justify the conclusion that a Hindu has a quick conscience or if he has it, he is so active as to charge him with moral indignation and drive him to undertake a crusade to eradicate the wrong. History shows that where ethics and economics come in conflict, victory is always with economics. Vested interests have never been known to have willingly diverted themselves unless there was sufficient force to compel them.

Untouchability is only an extended form of caste and therefore without abolition of caste, there is no hope of untouchability being vanished from the society. Untouchability has been in existence for the last two thousand years and during this period the Hindus have day in and day out mutilated the untouchables and trodden upon them in every way.

As far as the Hindus are concerned, untouchability is more than a religious system and it is a must for them. It is also an economic system which is worse than slavery. In slavery, the master at any rate has the responsibility to feed, clothe and house the slaves and keep them in good condition lest the market value of the slave should decrease. But in the system of untouchability, the Hindu takes no responsibility for the maintenance of the outcastes. As an economic system it permits exploitation without obligation. Untouchability is not only a system of unmitigated economic explosion, but also a system of uncontrolled exploitation. There is no check from the police or judiciary for the simple reason that they are all drawn from the Hindus and take the side of the exploiters.

Besides the shudras, the Hindu civilization has produced three social classes whose existence has not received the attention it deserves. The three classes are:

1. The criminal tribes
2. The aboriginal tribes.
3. The untouchables.

The existence of these classes is an abomination. The Hindu civilization gauged in the light of these social products could hardly be called a civilization. It is a diabolical contrivance to suppress and enslave humanity. Its proper name would be better called infamy. What else can be said of a civilization which has produced a mass of people who are taught to accept crime as an approved means of earning their livelihood, another mass of people who are left to live in full bloom of their primitive barbarism in the midst of civilization and a third mass of people who are treated as an entity beyond human intercourse and whose mere touch is enough to cause pollution?

The Hindu does not regard the existence of these classes as a matter of apology or shame and feels no responsibility to inquire into its origin and growth. On the other hand, every Hindu is taught to believe that his civilization is not only the most ancient but it is also in many respects altogether unique.

Today, all scholarships and awards and honour are confined to the brahmins and caste-Hindus and to their supporters and allies. But, unfortunately, no brahmin scholar has so far come forward to play the part of a Voltaire who had the intellectual honesty to rise against the doctrine of the Catholic Church in which he has been brought up nor is one likely to happen on the scene in the future. It is a grave reflection on the scholarship of the brahmins that they should not have produced a Voltaire. The brahmin scholar is only a learned man. He is not an intellectual. There is a world of difference between one who is learned and who is an intellectual. The former is class conscious and is alive to the interest of his class. The latter is an emancipated being who is free to act without being swayed by class consciousness. It is because the brahmins have been only learned men that they have not produced a Voltaire.

The selfish interest of a person or of the class to which he belongs always acts as an internal limitation which regulates the directions of his intellect. The power and position which the brahmins possess is entirely due to the Hindu civilization which treats them as supermen and subjects the outcastes to all sorts of disabilities so that they may never rise and challenge or threaten the superiority of the brahmins over them. Every brahmin is interested in the maintenance of brahmin supremacy whether he be orthodox or unorthodox, a priest or a *grahastha*, a scholar or not. How can the brahmins afford to be Voltaires? A Voltaire among the brahmins would be a positive danger to the maintenance of a civilization which is contrived to maintain brahmin supremacy. The intellect of a brahmin scholar is severely limited by his anxiety to preserve his interest. He suffers from his internal limitation as a result of which he does not allow his intellect full play which demands honesty and integrity. For he fears that it may affect the interest of his class and, therefore, his own.

What annoys one is the intolerance of the brahmin scholar towards any attempt to expose the Brahmanic literature. He himself would not play the part of an iconoclast even where it is necessary. And he would not allow a non-brahmin to have the capacity to do so. If any non-brahmin were to make such an attempt, the brahmin scholars would engage in a conspiracy of silence, take no notice of him, condemn him outright on some flimsy grounds or dub his work useless. The old orthodox Hindu does not think that there is anything wrong in the observance of untouchability but he is ashamed to discuss it in public for fear of letting the foreigner know that Hindu civilization can be guilty of such a vicious and infamous system or social code as evidenced by untouchability.[13]

Starting with the brahmins who form a strong and powerful element in the governing class in India, it is no exaggeration to say that they have been the most inveterate enemies of the servile classes, the shudras (the old name for

13. Dhananjay keer, *Life and Mission*, p. 271.

the non-brahmins), and the outcastes who together constitute about 85 per cent of the old Hindu population of India. If the common men belonging to the servile classes in India today feel so fallen; so degraded; so devoid of self-respect, hope, or ambition and so lifeless; it is entirely due to the brahmins and their philosophy.

The cardinal principles of this philosophy of Brahmanism were, to use a correct expression, six techniques of suppression:

1. graded inequality between the different classes;
2. complete discrimination of the shudras and the untouchables;
3. complete ban on the education of the shudras and the untouchables;
4. total exclusion of the shudras and the untouchables from the place of power and authority;
5. complete prohibition against the shudras and the untouchables acquiring property; and
6. complete subjugation and suppression of women.

Inequality is the official doctrine of Brahmanism, and the suppression of the outcastes aspiring to equality has been looked upon by them and carried out by them without remorse as their bounden duty. There are countries in the world where education did not spread beyond a few. But India is the only country where the intellectual class namely the brahmins not only made education their monopoly, but also declared acquisition of education by the outcastes, a crime punishable by cutting of the tongue or by the pouring of molten lead in the ear of the offender. The result is that for centuries the brahmins have denied the servile classes their right to education.

There is no social evil and no social wrong to which the brahmin has not given his support against the indigenous people. Manu's inhumanity to man such as the feeling of caste, untouchability, unapproachability and unseeability is a religion to the caste-Hindus. It would however, be a mistake to suppose that only the wrongs of man are a religion to the brahmins.

The brahmin has given his support to some of the worst wrongs that women have suffered from in any part of the world. In India, widows were burnt alive as *sati*s and the brahmin gave his fullest support to the practice. Widows were not allowed to remarry. The brahmins upheld the doctrine. Girls were required to be married before eight years of age and the husbands were permitted to claim the right to consummate or not, the marriage at any time after she had reached puberty. The brahmins defended the system.

The record of the brahmins as law-giver for the shudras, for the untouchables and for women, is the blackest as compared with the record of the intellectual classes in other parts of the world. For no intellectual class has prostituted its intelligence for the sole purpose of inventing a philosophy to keep its uneducated countrymen in a perpetual state of servility, ignorance and poverty as the brahmins have done in India.

Every brahmin today believes in this philosophy of Brahmanism propounded by his forefathers. He is an alien element in the Hindu society. There is a real gulf between him and the outcastes. He is not only alien to them but also hostile to them. In relationship between them there is in him no room for conscience and no call for justice. The caste-Hindus are very particular in treating the outcastes as traditional enemies but nowhere in the world there is a governing class as in India with such selfish, diseased and dangerous and perverse mentality with such a hideous and infamous philosophy of life which advocates the trampling down of the servile classes to sustain the power and glory of the governing class. In India, the governing class is a close corporation unwilling to admit anyone who does not belong to it by birth and ready to use every means to prevent the servile classes from rising to their level.

The Origin of Untouchability

The origin of untouchability is an enigma in modern history of India. It is the perverted outcome of the caste system. The Indo-Aryans divided themselves for different occupations on the basis of division of labour and according to aptitude, liking and capacity of the individuals. Those who took to learning were called brahmins. Those who undertook to governance were classified as kshatriyas, those who preferred to trade were called vaishyas and those who served the foregoing three class were known as shudras. But, in actual practice, this original principle of division of labour did not sustain itself long so much as even a most ignorant, vile and fallen brahmin continued to be regarded as someone next to God whereas a man from an outcaste, however, high in qualifications, was condemned for ever as a shudra. The result was that the original four divisions became watertight compartments and degenerated later into present caste system. In this way, the four *varnas* came to stay as four castes and the present tyrannous caste system became the reverse or the negation of its original meaning and purpose. Thereafter, different professions, barriers of provinces, varying ways of living, and diet, different superstitions and customs broke up the main four castes and further led to the creation of over three thousand sub-castes.

There is a view that the Aryans adopted this system to preclude the possibility of racial mixture with the original dwellers in India. As they did not accept the Indo-Aryans' suzerainty they led forays on their conquerors, kidnapped their children and women and harassed them by looting. In course of time, they were reduced to servile status, their arrivals in and departure from the villages were regulated. Unpleasant duties and insufferable disabilities were imposed upon them and in the end they were condemned as outcastes or untouchables.

There is another version that the untouchables originally were broken men and then followers of Buddhism. In their fallen days they did not assimilate themselves with the Vedic Hindus or give up beef eating and so they were degraded and segregated as untouchables. Ambedkar advances certain theories regarding the origin of untouchability:

1. There is no racial difference between the Hindus and the untouchables.
2. The distinction between the Hindus and untouchables in its original form before the advent of untouchability, was the distinction between tribesmen and broken men from alien tribes. It is the broken men who subsequently came to be treated as untouchables.
3. Just as untouchability has no racial basis, so also has it no occupational basis.
4. There are two roots from which untouchability has sprung —
   (a) contempt and hatred of the broken men as of Buddhist by brahmins; and
   (b) continuation of beef eating by the broken men after it had been given up by others.

5. Untouchables are distinct from impure.
6. While the impure as a class, came into existence at the time of Dharma-Sutra, the untouchables came into existence much later than CE 400.

On the part of the caste-Hindus, there was a contention that there were no sections of untouchables at all among the Hindus, realizing the danger of admitting the existence of untouchables. It was because a part of the privileges enjoyed by the caste-Hindus will have to be given up by them to the untouchables.

The caste-Hindus went to hide the historical truth that caste and untouchability are one integrated system based on one and the same principle. The idea of hoping to remove untouchability without destroying caste system is an utter futility. Caste system is a **diagnic** tree and untouchability is its shade. The people are now trying to remove the shadow retaining the tree there. Without cutting off the tree, how can this shade be removed. The reformers misguided idea is founded on fallacy. The two are one and in-separable. Untouchability is only an extension of the caste system. The two stand together and will fall together.

Untouchability will vanish only when the whole of the Hindu social order, particularly the caste system, will be dissolved. The sanction for the caste system derives from the Vedas which form the sacred book of the Hindu religion and which are infallible. To a Hindu, caste is sacred and eternal.

The intellectuals realize that caste is only an instrument for exploitation and discrimination of the downtrodden. The discrimination against the outcastes is practised by the caste-Hindus on a scale the extent of which is impossible for an outsider to imagine. The best example for discrimination can be explained thus: A caste-Hindu singer is described as a great

Indian singer. If the same person happens to be an outcaste he would be described as an untouchable singer. If a caste-Hindu leader happens to be an untouchable, he would be described as an untouchable leader.

This type of discrimination has its origin in the Hindu view that the outcastes are inferior people. However qualified and great the outcastes are, they are only great among the untouchables. They can never be greater nor even equal to the great men among the caste-Hindus.

The discrimination against the outcastes is merely the reflection of that deep and strong Hindu sentiment. Those discriminations have their roots in the fear of the Hindus, that in a free field, the outcastes may rise above the prescribed status in life and become a menace to the Hindu social order, the cardinal principle of which is the maintenance of Hindu superiority and Hindu domination over the outcastes. So long as the Brahmanical social order lasts, discrimination against the outcastes will continue to exist.

Main help us "We must have a government in which the men in power will give their undivided allegiance to the best interest of the country. We must have a government in which men in power, knowing where obedience will end and the resistance will begin, will not be afraid to amend the social and economic code of life which will dictate the principles of justice and expediency so urgently call for. This role the British government played for centuries. It is only a government which is of the people, for the people, and by the people that will make this possible."

> ". . . we feel that nobody can remove our grievances and we cannot remove them unless we get political power in our own hands. No share of this political power can evidently come to us so long as the British government remains as it

> is. It is only in a Swaraj Constitution that we stand any change of getting the political power into our own hands, without which we cannot bring salvation to our people.
>
> "The depressed classes feel that they will get no share of the political power, unless the political machinery for the new constitution is of a special make. In the construction of that machine, certain hard facts of Indian social life must not be lost sight of. It must be recognized that Indian society is a gradation of castes forming an ascending scale of reverence and a descending scale of contempt — a system which gives no scope for the growth of that sentiment of equality and fraternity so essential for a democratic form of government."[14]
>
> ". . . All I say at the present moment is that although we want responsible government we do not want a government that will only mean a change of masters."[15]

Ambedkar was not interested in merely shouting slogans against the British Rule but he also attacked the British rule vehemently with hard words in the Round Table Conference. The most important work he did to achieve his goal was the presentation of the declaration of the fundamental rights of the depressed classes. He prepared a scheme with great labour and statesmanship and submitted it to the Minorities Sub-Committee for being included in the future Constitution of India.[16]

History Behind the Constitutional Rights of the Untouchables

The untouchables being the ignored humanity in India, caught in the fire of caste system and untouchability for thousands of years perishing under the feet of Brahmanism, were fighting

14. Ibid., p. 271.
15. D.D. Kosambi, *Culture and Civilization of Ancient India*.
16. Dhananjay Keer, op. cit., p. 272.

tooth and nail for their emancipation. The last phase of their fight was for their constitutional safeguards instead of mere verbal promises.

When Ambedkar had the occasion to draft the Constitution for India, he insisted on enlisting in the Constitution various measures for the emancipation of the downtrodden. The drafting of the Constitution was completed by 1949, except a chapter on the Scheduled Castes (SCs) and Scheduled Tribes (STs). That chapter became a controversial matter. Ambedkar being the Chairman of the Drafting Committee and also the undisputed leader of the depressed classes raised the question of reservation of rights for the SCs and STs. He demanded only a small percentage of rights for the SCs and STs in the place of cent-per-cent reservation of rights enjoyed by the caste-Hindus and their co-travellers.

It was the irony of history of India that the great Gandhi was dead against the principle of separate safeguards for the SCs and STs, which ended in the "epic fast unto death." When Ambedkar demanded inclusion of the clauses in the Constitution for safeguarding the interests of the untouchables by reservation, some of the top leaders of the struggle for Indian Independence, who were also members of the Drafting Committee had vehemently and stubbornly opposed the proposal. It was not a secret that behind the protest was Gandhi. But Ambedkar was not astonished at the stand taken by the people's leaders because he knew that it was a continuation of the "war" waged at the Round Table Conference. Ambedkar was for so many years experiencing the mentality and attitude of the Brahmanical section towards the depressed classes. It is a continuation of the enmity of Brahmanism for thousands of years towards the outcastes.

Babasaheb Ambedkar argued with the members who were against the policy of reservation to include a chapter on the reservation of rights for the depressed classes but all in vain. Nobody took a lenient attitude. Finding no other solution, as a last step, he, the Chairman of the Drafting Committee, absented himself from the Constituent Assembly for three consecutive days. That was a silent but vehement protest of a single man's war for the interests of the outcastes.

There were twenty-nine members for the SCs and STs in the Constituent Assembly. But it was a pity that they as a single man acted like machine soldiers of Mahatma Gandhi. They were to dance to the tune of Brahmanism by sheer fear of attacks from their traditional masters in case they supported Ambedkar. S.N. Shastri who was a close friend and follower of Ambedkar, approached each and everyone of the twenty seven members of the depressed classes to convince them of the grave situation and of the importance and seriousness of Ambedkar's silent protest but to the shame of the entire population of the depressed classes, nobody could be moved to the side of Ambedkar, even though they were aware of the importance of the stand taken by the Chairman of the Drafting Committee. Every Dalit member of the Constituent Assembly deceived Ambedkar.

S.N. Shastri had revealed these facts in an article published in a contemporary periodical in 1969 (*Dhamma Deep Special*, 1969, pp. 41-45). It was interesting to note that the media run by the caste-Hindus refused to publish that article and give publicity to that historical fact as it was against the interest of the non-Dalits.

The members in question were alive when these facts were revealed to the public but nobody had the courage to deny these facts. Even Jawaharlal Nehru never dared to refute the allegation.

When Ambedkar came out victorious from his "one man's war," in securing constitutional sanction for the right of reservation, those members of the outcastes began to fight one by one on the same line to have a right of self-determination for the outcastes. They might have felt pinpricking of conscience as they could not lend their ears to the voice of history at the appropriate time.

When Ambedkar took a resolute stand, applying his sharp weapon of non-cooperation, Jawaharlal Nehru, Shyama Prasad Mukherji and Sardar Patel, realized the gravity and value of Ambedkar's silent but meaningful protest without uttering a word. Then only they dared to make a clear understanding on the problem with Ambedkar. As a result of their capitulation and compromise the Articles on SCs and STs were allowed to be included in the Draft Constitution.[17]

From the above facts, it is as clear as daylight that the constitutional rights that the SCs and STs and backward classes are enjoying now were obtained not merely out of generosity or magnanimity of anybody. Those rights were achieved by the relentless and unremitting labour of their saviour Ambedkar and his activities, when most of the other leaders from the depressed classes were hitting at his back with the encouragement and support of the enemies of the Dalits. Had he not been there as the Chairman of the Drafting Committee of the Constitution of India, the welfare of the SCs and STs and backward communities and other weaker sections of the society would have been a mere dream when the political powers were captured by the stronger sections.

When one dares to evaluate all these facts of history, it can be concluded that the modern history of the Dalits of India began with Bhim Rao Ambedkar.

---

17. Ambedkar, op. cit., III, p. 41.

2

Economic Philosophy of Dr Babasaheb Ambedkar

Architect of the Indian Constitution

Ambedkar's contributions to the framing of the Indian Constitution are too well known to be repeated and still, no writings on him would be complete without mentioning one of his greatest contributions. He brought to bear on the task that was entrusted to him as the Chairman of the Drafting Committee of the Indian Constitution, a vast array of qualities — scholarship, imagination, logic and experience. The Indian Constitution as drafted by him aims at blending political democracy with social and economic democracy. It is noteworthy that the Constituent Assembly has recorded, "words fail to convey the gratitude for the legal acumen, the untiring industry, the consummate skill and firmness tempered with moderation with which Ambedkar piloted the Constitution." The debates of the Constituent Assembly contain such lucid expositions on the interpretation of the provisions of the Constitution that it is not surprising that even today when questions on the interpretation of the Constitution arise, eminent jurists turn to Ambedkar's contemporaneous exposition of the Constitution.

The view taken by the founding fathers of the Constitution under the leadership of Ambedkar was that the Constitution should not only prescribe the political structure of society but also define and guarantee its social and economic ideals. Ambedkar felt that even in a democracy, leaving social matters to be determined exclusively by a political majority could lead to the dictatorship of the "haves" and perpetuations of age-long social tyranny. He, therefore, wanted the economic and social objectives to be enshrined in the Constitution itself. Hence, the incorporation of not only the Fundamental Rights but also the Directive Principles in our Constitution.

The abiding concern of Ambedkar for the principles of justice, equality, liberty and fraternity was enshrined in the preamble to the Constitution of India thus:

> We must make our political democracy a social democracy as well. Political democracy cannot last, unless there lies at the base of it, social democracy. What does social democracy mean? It means a way of life which recognized liberty, equality and fraternity as the principles of life. Liberty cannot be divorced from equality; equality cannot be divorced from liberty. Nor can liberty and equality be divorced from fraternity. Without equality, liberty will produce the supremacy of the few over the many. Equality without liberty will kill the individual initiative. Without fraternity, liberty and equality could not become a natural course of things. . . . We must begin by acknowledging the fact that there is complete absence of two things in Indian society: one of these is equality. The second is recognition of fraternity. Fraternity means a sense of common brotherhood of all Indians being one people. It is the principle which give unity and solidarity to social life. It is a difficult thing to achieve. Without fraternity, equality and liberty will be no deeper than a coat of paint.

The Indian Constitution, as set out in the Preamble, is a testament to secure to all its citizens Justice, Liberty, Equality and Fraternity. The Constitution guarantees the Fundamental Rights of the citizens, especially equality, freedom of speech and expression, protection of life and liberty, non-discrimination, freedom of religion, abolition of untouchability and prohibition of forced labour. The Directive Principles of State Policy envisage a social order in which justice: social, economic, and political, will be ensured in all institutions of national life; inequalities will be removed with provision for adequate means of livelihood, equitable control and ownership of material resources of the community, protection of interests of the weaker sections of the society, particularly the SCs and the STs. Almost all the issues which confront the poor and also any citizen or any other individual in their daily lives find place in the Constitution, whether it is equality, freedom, human dignity, non-discrimination, social and economic justice, right to livelihood, right to work, living wage or protection from exploitation. The Constitution is a fabric cover around a just and equitable society. The credit for incorporation of all these vital aspects ensuring equality and dignity of individuals obviously goes to Ambedkar.

A Crusader for Social Justice

It would be necessary to recall the oft-quoted but inimitable words of Ambedkar in his final address to the Constituent Assembly wherein he drew attention to the emerging contradictions in the society of free India.

> On the social plane, we have in India, a society based on the principles of graded inequality which means elevation of some and degradation for others. On the economic plane, we have a society in which there are some who have immense wealth as against many who live in abject poverty. On the 26 January 1950, we are going to enter into a life of contradictions. In politics, we will have equality. In social and economic life, we will have inequality. In politics, we will be recognizing the principle of one man one vote and one vote one value. In our social and economic life, we shall,

> by reason of our social and economic structure, continue to deny the principle of one man one value. How long shall we continue to live this life of contradictions? How long shall we continue to deny it? We will do so only by putting our political democracy in peril. We must remove this contradiction at the earliest possible moment; or else, those who suffer from inequality, will blow up the structure of political democracy which this Assembly has laboriously built up.[1]

This clearly indicates the ardent desire of Ambedkar to establish social and economic democracy consistent with political democracy.

Ambedkar saw the Indian caste system as a serious obstacle in the path of democracy, equality and justice. For him the caste system was a specifically Indian expression of institutionalized inequality and indignity, with elevation for some and degradation for others. The abolition of untouchability was a significant Constitutional provision for securing human dignity to the Dalits and a positive step towards equality and social justice.

It would appear on the one hand that the State has put in place laws and programmes without which even the limited change in the overall situation of social disabilities could not have been possible; on the other hand, these measures are too poorly implemented.

Ambedkar was a social revolutionary and a relentless champion of human rights. His major concern throughout his life was at establishing equal status to all classes, in social, economic and political arena offering an opportunity to all to rise in the scale of life and creating conditions for their advancement. His struggle for the SC emanated from the belief

1. Bhagwan Das, *Relevance of Ambedkar*, p. 7.

that India, as a society could not achieve any progress, if a large segment of the society remained oppressed and is not allowed to realize its potential. According to Ambedkar, stability was needed but not at the cost of social justice. He said on one occasion, "White washing does not save a dilapidated house. You must pull it down and build anew."

Ambedkar was a great scholar. His prolific writings bear testimony to his scholarship in diverse areas like sociology, anthropology, history, economics, politics, law and religion. Ambedkar firmly believed that education held the key to social and economic upliftment of the downtrodden. Besides imploring them to educate themselves, Ambedkar actively helped the cause by establishing several educational institutions.

It is sad to note that caste-related violence is still occurring, despite several protective legislations. Hence, there is perhaps a need for stricter implementation of the constitutional safeguards. More than the laws and State action, it would appear that the society itself has to accept and imbibe the value of equality, non-discrimination and democratic behaviour. For this, the mindset of the people must change. What's at stake is the dignity of the human individual. As Ambedkar himself observed.

> Democracy is not merely a form of government. It is essentially an attitude of respect and reverence towards fellowmen.[2]

Although some measure of social and economic progress has indeed been made during the last half century, nevertheless more people than ever before, find themselves at the dawn of the new millennium in a state of abysmal poverty.

2. Gadekar, *Socio-Economic Thoughts of Ambedkar*, Vice-Chancellor, Ambedkar University, Lucknow.

Notwithstanding six decades and nine five-year plans since the commencement of the Constitution, there is widespread poverty, exploitation and inequality in the country. Though the proportion of the poor people below the poverty line — the cut-off line between the poor and the non-poor — has shown a drop if the official reports are to be believed, the total number of poor has almost doubled, in terms of absolute numbers. There is therefore a need to vigorously implement the programmes advocated by Ambedkar to ameliorate the conditions in which the poor live.

An Eminent Economist

GENERAL PROBLEMS OF ECONOMY

It is universally acknowledged that the general problems of the Indian economy are indeed serious. Mounting unemployment, rising number of poor people, growing social tensions, concentration of resources in the hands of a few, lack of proper distribution of income, negligible access of marginalized sections to public facilities, labour unrest, gender-based discriminations, pitiable living conditions of urban slum dwellers, SCs and STs, agriculture-industry mismatch, failures in the land reforms sector, faster population growth and lack of moral values are some of the issues of concern in our economy. Ambedkar tried his best to raise these issues from time to time on every platform. Records show that Ambedkar with his academic knowledge of subjects like economics, political science, Constitution and law contributed to the evolution of a development. His life and career were fully dedicated to key socio-economic issues which the nation is facing even today.

Even after six decades of Independence, we are facing the basic economic problems such as poverty, unemployment, slow rate of growth, slow rate of industrialization, unequal distribution of national income, low productivity in agriculture, etc.

The Indian economy, even today, is mainly rural-based where inequitable land distribution, semi-feudal labour relations, constraints on extension of the Green Revolution, improper linkages of agricultural and industrial sectors and disguised unemployment are observed.

GLOBALIZATION OF ECONOMY

To overcome the various problems faced by the country, the Government of India had taken several measures for liberalization and globalization of the economy since 1991. Trade and industrial policies have been further liberalized and various monetary and fiscal measures have been initiated to supplement trade policies. The views of Ambedkar on fiscal and monetary systems and their influence on growth of industry, price stability, external debt, etc. and their relevance in the present context deserve detailed analysis.

Ambedkar's book *The Problem of the Rupee — Its Origin and its Solution* was considered an instructive treatise on a controversial subject. He advocated that the standard of value should be gold and the elasticity of the currency should come from this source. Ambedkar mainly dealt with monetary standards as they had evolved during a few decades. The Indian Rupee until 1893 was linked to silver standard, meaning that the Indian rupee was based on the value of the silver contained in it. Due to enormous silver discoveries subsequently, the price of silver fell and hence the price of rupee slipped also in terms of gold. From 1872 to 1893, the decline in price of silver led to automatic devaluation of the rupee. While devaluation helped Indian exports, it was bad for the country's economy as we had to pay in gold, which was the currency in England (Gold Sterling). Subsequently, the gold standard was established in 1906 in England. However the system broke down in 1916 with the enormous rise in the price of silver and the system effectively became the silver standard. Ambedkar argued for a proper gold standard with gold currency, as he was highly critical of the gold exchange standard. Ambedkar argued that this system vested the government with enormous power to increase the money supply. The excessive importance given to maintain the stability of exchange as against internal stability of the value of currency was not a proper policy for India. Ambedkar effectively argued that the low exchange rate increased exports and boosted internal prices, which benefited the trading classes at the expense of the poor people at home. Ambedkar emphasized "what really concerns those who use money is not how much gold that money is worth, but how much of things in general that money is stable in terms of commodities in general, and what matters to the welfare of people is not so much the precious metals as commodities and services of more direct utility."[3] Ambedkar's commitment obviously was for internal stability of prices. In short, Ambedkar's conclusion is clearly towards price stability through conservative and automatic monetary management.

Ambedkar's views are extremely relevant, in these days of massive budget deficits and their automatic monetization. It would appear that we could do with an effective restraint on liquidity creation through an automatic mechanism. Today we have no gold or gold exchange standard. The whole perspective had undergone a sea-change. However, we can

---

3. *Dr Ambedkar's Contribution to the Indian Economics,* Ambedkar Memorial Lectures-II delivered by Pref S. Ambirajan, Honorary Professor of Economics, Madras School of Economics, Chennai.

still take lessons from his economic philosophy. For instance, during later years of 1980s and even in early 2000s, the rupee had depreciated in relation to major currencies so much so that it seriously affected the credit rating of India. This was also the period of high prices. Thus, we find that currency was issued in excess, resulting in fall in the purchasing power locally and the depreciation of the rupee internationally. This is exactly the situation visualized by Ambedkar. A strict control on issue of currency was what Ambedkar advised in those days, which is exactly what we need today.[4] Ambedkar obviously had shown great scholarship and hard work in this book which received wide acclaim from his contemporaries as an incisive study of the currency problem of the Indian subcontinent.

ADMINISTRATION AND FINANCE OF THE EAST INDIA COMPANY

Ambedkar dealt with the finances of East India Company in his work *Administration and Finance of the East India Company* and disagreed with the entire fiscal system under the regime of the East India Company. Ambedkar believed that the finances of a country are to be judged from the point of view of developmental expenditure, the public works benefiting the entire community taking an important place. Ambedkar observed that the surplus generated by East India Company were not used to undertake irrigation and other works of improvement and were used to pay dividends to the East India Company's shareholders; and as the flow of money from India was not sufficient to pay the dividends, the East India Company was resorting to heavy public debt. Ambedkar felt that this large size of the debt was the result of mismanagement and extravagance by the Company. He also

4. M.L. Kasare, *Economic Philosophy of Ambedkar.*

opined that while heavy land tax levied by East India Company prevented the prosperity of the agricultural sector, the custom taxes and heavy export duties hampered the growth of trade and industry, and the goods produced in the country were unable to meet the external competition.[5] Ambedkar came down very heavily on the taxation policy of the government by stating that:

> The landlords who passed their lives in conspicuous consumption and vicarious leisure on the earnings of the poor tenants, and the many European civil servants were supremely exempted from any contribution towards the maintenance of the government. On the other hand, the salt tax and tax on trades and occupations embracing weavers, carpenters, all workers in metals, all salesmen or vendors by the road-side, etc. extending to the most trifling articles of trade and the cheapest tools mechanics can employ, and other oppressive taxes continued to harass the industrious poor.[6]

Ambedkar also examined how the revenues raised through such taxes were spent. He observed that education formed no part of the expenditure and useful public works were lamentably few.[7] He found that during 1809-57, the military expenditure accounted for more than half of the total revenues, without benefiting the general public of India. Ambedkar concluded the collapse of imperial system was due to a faulty fiscal system, indiscriminate taxes and unproductive and extravagant expenditure.[8]

---

5. Babasaheb Ambedkar, *Writings and Speeches*, Government of Maharashtra, vol. 6, 1989.
6. Ibid., p. 78.
7. Ibid., p. 83.
8. Ibid.

EVOLUTION OF PROVINCIAL FINANCE IN BRITISH INDIA

In his thesis on *The Evolution of Provincial Finance in British India* (1926) Ambedkar clearly expressed his views about the decentralization of economic power and its relevance to public finances. Ambedkar examined the fiscal policy adopted by the Government of India and the financial relationship between Imperial and Provincial Governments during 1833 to 1919. Ambedkar discussed the development of Provincial Finance in three parts, viz. Budget by Assignment, Budget for Assigned Revenues and Budget-shared Revenues. After tracing the development of Provincial Finance, stage by stage, Ambedkar brings out the fact that the Provincial Finance was not independent prior to 1919. By the Act of 1833, the revenues became, by law, the revenues of the Government of India. The provinces became the collecting and spending agencies of the Government, of India. They ceased to levy any new taxes or to collect the old in their own name.[9]

The Reforms Act of 1919 provided for the first time a clear demarcation of administrative and financial matters between Central and Provincial Governments. Ambedkar, after examining the new provisions of the Act 1919, was quite straightforward in his attack, when he stated that the "whole policy of India has been dictated by the interests of English manufacturers is beyond dispute."[10] Ambedkar forcefully advocated the need "for sound government for sound finances." Ambedkar advocated that the provinces could have undertaken reduction of expenditure and increase in taxation, which is very necessary for soundness of the system. Ambedkar pointed out that "if there is no sound finance in

9. Ibid.
10. Ibid., Evolution of Provincial Finance in British India, Government of Maharashtra.

the Provinces, there cannot be a sound financial system in the country and where there is no good system of finance . . ."[11] This could go down, as one of the most perceptive comments ever made on the disastrous political experiment introduced in colonial India by the British.

The main point Ambedkar tried to make in short is that an alien government cannot be expected to use the funds it possess for the betterment of the people. As Ambedkar made it clear:

> If the Executive in India did not do certain things most conducive to progress, it was because by reason of its being impersonal and also by reason of its charactrer, motives and interests it could sympathize with the living forces operating in the Indian society, was not charged with its wants, its pains, its craving and its desires, was inimical to its aspirations, did not advance education, disfavoured Swadeshi or snapped at anything that smacked of nationalism, it was because all those things went against its grain.

In other words, the government, "not being of the people could not feel the pulse of the people." Ambedkar had the courage of conviction to criticize the government policies in a forthright manner, while we were still under foreign yoke. Ambedkar analysed the consequences of the Montague-Chelmsford Reforms on provincial finance and cited the communication from the Secretary of State written in 1922 which stated "if the financial stability of the provinces is not to be undermined, with ultimate jeopardy to the Government of India itself, it is impossible to contemplate the continuance of a series of provincial deficits financed by borrowing either direct from the public or from the Central Government."[12]

11. Ibid.
12. K. Raghvendra Rao, *Babasaheb Ambedkar, Economic Ideas.*

The Secretary of State went on to add that "Equlibrium can only be achieved by reduction of expenditure and the adoption of measures which will lead to an increase in revenue." Years later in 1939, Ambedkar remarked that "patriotism vanishes when you touch a man's pocket and I am sure that the states representatives will prefer their own financial interests to the necessities of a common front."[13] This leads us to conclude that Ambedkar squarely blamed the State Governments for lacking the will to achieve efficient and equitable economic administration. It is therefore necessary that the Government organize and marshall the national resources to build up the national wealth and not by borrowing from the public or from the Central Government. If enough revenue is not generated, the fault lies with the State Governments. Indeed, what Ambedkar commented in 1939 is true to some extent of the Indian Government.[14]

TAXATION

Ambedkar knew clearly the problems in levy of taxes. He pointed out that it is very difficult to have proper taxation policies as the governments which depend on the people's vote to govern would be always hesistant to mobilize the needed resources through requisite taxation and at the same time the government cannot take measures to reduce public expenditure by enforcing administrative economics. Ambedkar has effectively summarized the position by stating, if however, "the seat is a gift of the elector, a candidate to the Legislature who proposes to touch his pocket has a small chance of success,

13. *Dr. Ambedkar's Contribution to the Indian Economics*, Ambedkar Memorital Lectures-II delivered by Professor S. Ambirajan, Honorary Professor of Economics, Madras School of Economics, Chennai.

14. Ibid.

even though the new taxes are to result in more than proportionate benefit." In any case a political party which "has won power from a bureaucracy by accusing it of heavy taxation cannot easily disgrace itself by continuing the same policy." The result was that "the chances of an early equilibrium in provincial finance are very small." Though Ambedkar expressed these views in 1939, one wonders whether Ambedkar was talking of the present status of state finances in India.

Having analysed the evaluation of public finances in provinces, Ambedkar never missed any opportunity to comment on the existing taxation policy and suggested an alternative tax policy. Ambedkar's views on taxation were included in the election manifesto of his Independent Labour Party (1936). Ambedkar had criticized the Government of Bombay at a public meeting held in Ahmedabad in 1938 for not reducing the land tax rates and for not taxing the rich people. The following are the important components of the taxation policy advocated by Ambedkar:[15]

(a) A personal tax should be based on taxable capacity of the individual and not on his gross income;

(b) Tax rates should be progressive, meaning the rich should be taxed more and the poor less; and

(c) There should be exemptions subject to a limit of income tax for taxpayers.

Ambedkar had shown considerable concern about using taxation policy for reducing income inequalities between different sections of people. According to him, taxes should help to achieve relative equity between different sections of people. He has also argued that, "no taxation system should

---

15. O.D. Heggade, *Economic Thought of Ambedkar*, p. 73.

be manipulated as to lower the standard of living of the people."[16]

Power to States to Levy Taxes

Ambedkar has identified that the provinces had come to rely on grants-in-aid from the Central Government in British India. He considered it a fiscal imbalance. Ambedkar argued in favour of provincial governments retaining the power of sales tax, since it is an important source of their revenue. Ambedkar had argued in the Constitution Assembly that:

> If we permit the sales tax to be levied by the provinces, then the provinces must be free to adjust the rate of the sales tax to the changing situation of the provinces, and therefore a ceiling from the centre would be a great handicap in the working of the sales tax. The sales tax in its fundamental character must be a tax on consumption.[17]

Ambedkar was in favour of imposing an estate tax. He suggested it as a measure of achieving economic equity. A similar proposal was made by Nicholas Kaldor, a former British economist in his *Integrated Tax Structure for India.* This recommendation was accepted but the Government of India had abolished it subsequently.

One of the criticisms of Ambedkar about the provincial finances was that the allocation for social services by the provincial governments was inadequate, which criticism still perhaps holds good, looking at the level of poverty in the country. He was also against more allocation for army and defence purposes.

APPOINTMENT OF FINANCE COMMISSION

Ambedkar enunciated the principles of Centre-State financial

16. Ambedkar, *Constituent Assembly Debates*, vol. 10, p. 339.
17. Ibid.

relations in the Constitution of India keeping in view the need for a strong Centre and the proximity of State Governments to the people based on his analysis titled *The Evolution of Provincial Finances in British India.*

Ambedkar was in favour of a strong Central Government keeping in view the needs of nation-building. The revenue-raising powers and development responsibilities were unequally distributed between the Union Government and State Governments in India since 1947. This has been an important problem in Centre-State financial relations in modern India.

Nine Finance Commissions have so far submitted their reports and the Tenth Finance Commission is about to complete its task. The provision for appointment of Finance Commission itself is a contribution from Ambedkar.[18] Even after six decades, the financial relations between the Centre and States remain unrectified; and the latter continues to depend on the Centre for financial support to some extent. The reason, *inter alia,* is the inability of the States to reduce expenditure on unproductive works. Ambedkar stated that the pressure of development and taxation was bound to increase but the problem of distribution of burden among various governments had not been taken care of.

The main conclusions of Ambedkar are probably more relevant now than they were at the time he wrote, if one looks at the State and Central deficit finances. The main objective of public fiscal system according to Ambedkar was to make administrative policies independent by requiring them to finance their programmes from their own resources without depending upon other sources.

---

18. Ibid., vol. 10., p. 340.

FISCAL DEFICIT

Briefly stated, a deficit budget is one where the estimated expenditure is in excess of receipts. In a well-managed financial system the capital expenditure is, to a large extent, to be met from out of the savings of the revenue budget which means that the revenue expenditure has to be less than the revenue receipts. But generally the entire capital expenditure is never met by the revenue surplus alone. There is always a borrowing (within the country and abroad) to finance capital expenditure in addition to the revenue surplus. When the total expenditure is partly met out of borrowing, it leads to deficit.

Is deficit financing desirable or not? There is no straightforward "yes" or "no" answer to this. Deficit financing is good under certain circumstances and is not so under some other circumstances.

Deficit financing itself is not bad provided the loans taken to finance the budget deficit are properly spent in the sense that the debt capital is spent on projects which will yield returns to repay the loans. However, the returns are charges recovered from users of the projects and, in real politics, not many state governments or Central Government are willing to operate a state or country's economy on the commercial lines as there are issues of public policy which dictate differential pricing and subsidies due to flagrant income inequalities. Thus, subsidies are good from an egalitarian point of view. But bad implementation of subsidy policy is neither in favour of nor in the interest of efficient financial management. To give just one example, if in an economy the people below the poverty line are 30 per cent and the food subsidy is given to 80 per cent of the population, it is a wrong way of targeting poverty and a clear instance of wasteful expenditure. Similarly, deficit financing even to undertake capital projects like irrigation, power and roads, by itself, does not contribute to stable finance if the charges recovered from users do not cover repayment of the interest and principal besides operation and maintenance costs, etc.

Need to Reduce Non-productive Expenditure

Majority of States in India are on the verge of over-utilizing the overdraft facility sanctioned by the Reserve Bank, and the position in some States has assumed such serious proportions that the State treasuries are required to be closed and financial relief packages have to be worked out to meet the financial crisis. It is necessary for the States to take measures to increase the tax revenue and to reduce the non-productive expenditure. The overdraft is essentially a facility the Reserve Bank extends to the States which allows them to issue cheques even when they have no funds in their bank account. The number of days all States were in overdraft mode was 954 days in the first six months of 2000-01, which rose to 1222 during the same period in 2001-02, a hike of 28 per cent as per the latest reports. The obvious reasons for this state of affairs have been that the State Governments have not been able to raise the necessary resources to fund their expenditure and the populist nature of their policies. The states are finding it increasingly difficult to pay salaries, service debts and invest in infrastructure and the social sector. The outstanding debt of all the States taken together has more than doubled from Rs.2,43,000 crore in March 1997 to about Rs.5,00,000 crore in March 2001. The interest liabilities of the States rose sixfold during the 1990s and stands at Rs.54,000 crore. None of the States have come to terms with this harsh reality, which will only worsen the situation in the near future.

NEED FOR MOBILIZATION OF INTERNAL RESOURCES

If one analyses the enormous difficulties of the Government of India as well as the State Governments, one would be appalled at the manner in which the governments have been mobilizing additional resources from the financial and multilateral institutions to bridge the budget deficit rather than mobilizing the national resources though taxation, cutting down subsidies and limiting subsidies only for target groups of the weaker sections of the society. Both the Government of India and State Governments have been resorting to heavy borrowings to meet the deficit budget. It happens year after year which has led to a virtual debt trap. If one looks at the Budget for 2001-02 of the Government of India, which depicts, *inter alia,* revenue deficit of about Rs.80,000 crore and fiscal deficit of over Rs.1,11,000 crore the enormity of the problem becomes evident. We also continue to borrow about Rs.1,16,000 crore to make interest payment of Rs.1,12,000 crore signifying that we are borrowing even to pay the interest on loans taken over a period of time.[19] This state of affairs is a reflection of very poor management of our finances. The finances of the States would be no better and in many cases it may be even worse. In this context, the views of Ambedkar are more relevant today than at a time when these views were expressed.

PRINCIPLES GOVERNING EXPENDITURE OF GOVERNMENT

During the discussion on the functions of the Comptroller and Auditor-General, Ambedkar at the time of framing the Constitution in 1949, had enunciated that governments should spend the resources mobilized from the public not only as per rules and regulations, but also to ensure that "faithfulness, wisdom and economy" have gone into the acts of expenditure by public authorities. It is necessary for the government to recognize that the main reason for the existence of public finance is to utilize these funds for creating common facilities and

19. M.L. Kasare, op. cit.

services used by the society like roads, etc. As the cost and benefit analysis of such items cannot easily be worked out, it will not be possible for the private sector to provide such facilities for the common man. The government is expected to take judicious decisions in taking up such works, which would give maximum benefit for maximum number of people. Care should also be taken not only in allocating funds for common facilities, but also in spending such funds objectively without frittering away on wasteful expenditure. Hence, it becomes all the more necessary for the government to be faithful to the original intentions. The expenditure must be committed with circumspection and understanding of the deeper issues involved in public expenditure. It does not simply mean a low level of public spending, but it is the intelligent use of funds so that every paisa fetches the maximum benefit. Those in charge of public funds must strive to evaluate alternative methods of achieving the objectives and see to it that leakages do not occur. The government should ensure that the expenditure decisions are closely related to the specified objectives and the available resources besides ensuring economy, efficiency and effectiveness in the implementation of government decisions. In the present context of high fiscal deficits, a rigorous application of the principles enunciated by Ambedkar can help moderate the quantum of public expenditure and utilization of limited resources in a need-based and judicious manner.

ECONOMIC REFORMS

As an economist Ambedkar always remained preoccupied with the well-being of the common man. Several of his economic writings bore an eloquent testimony to his concern for the common man. According to him, the well-being of the common man could be secured, among other things, through the State planning the economic life of the society and not leaving it to the whims of the market alone; by ensuring domestic price stability as inflation hits the poor most. The poor are not adversely affected through incidence of taxation. The expenditure policy of the government should be so framed that the quantum of productive expenditure is enhanced and the unproductive expenditure is curtailed to the barest minimum.

Ambedkar wanted the expenditure policy of the State government to be guided, among other things, by the principle of providing more public utility services as also generating more employment. It is necessary to analyse the expenditure pattern of the Government of India during the post-economic reforms period in this context.

India initiated wide-ranging economic reforms since 1991 encompassing almost all the sectors of the economy. The thrust of the reforms is to transform the planned economy into a market-driven economy which, through competition and efficiency, would help the country secure higher rate of economic growth. Under the circumstances, the role of the States in the overall economic development gets severely restricted. The role of the State would be confined largely to provide the people, particularly the poor, with social services such as education, health and sanitation, subsidized food and so on. It would be worthwhile to examine as to what has really been happening to the expenditure on social services.

It is observed that the food subsidy, a major component of assistance in a poverty stricken country like ours, has more or less remained at the same level of Rs.15,000 crore to about Rs. 20,000 crore the over the last decade(1991-92 to 2001-02). The so-called subsidy is mostly diverted to meeting increased buffer stocks carrying costs and no tangible benefit has accrued to the poor. In the recent years, the public distribution prices are more or less at par with market prices. Expenditure on health in general and public health in particular did not show any significant increase between 1992-93 and 1997-98. The same is the case with the expenditure on rural family welfare. Expenditure on education witnessed a marginal increase. But expenditure on child and women development, with exceptions of 1995-96 and 1996-97, remained stagnant. Rural employment appears to be the biggest casualty of the reforms. Expenditure on it remained almost stable, average being Rs. 1331 crore during 1993-94 to 1996-97 and declined to around Rs. 900 crore in the last two years. Same is the case with the Jawahar Rozgar Yojna and the IDRP.

> There is not much noticeable increase in the expenditure on SC/ST welfare. Lastly taking into consideration total expenditure of the Central Government on all social services, employment generation and poverty alleviation programmes it is observed that it increased by around 2200 crore during 1990-91 to 1992-93 and remained stagnant in the 1995-96 level. On the other hand, there has been a sustained increase in the interest payments between 1991-92 and 1995-96. Though they are slightly lower in 1996-97 and 1997-98 compared to 1995-96 level, they are about Rs. 2000 crore to Rs. 2200 crore higher than in 1991-92.[20]

Further the expenditure on social services in percentage of GDP does not show any major increase. For instance, the food subsidy declined from around 0.45 per cent of GDP in 1990-91 to 0.39 per cent in 1992-93, increased to 0.64 per cent in 1993-94 and then continuously declined for the rest of the period. The expenditure on general health and public health stagnated at mere 0.09 per cent and 0.03 per cent respectively. The same is the case with rural family welfare and maternal and child health.

---

20. Budget of 2001-02, Govt. of India.

But the most disturbing scenario appears to be in respect of employment generation and poverty-alleviation schemes. The aggregate expenditure on all social services and employment-oriented and poverty alleviation programmes remained just 1.87 per cent of the GDP in 1997-98 as it was in 1990-91, obviously with some minor annual fluctuations. On the other hand, expenditure on interest payments alone is not only twice or even two and half times higher than total expenditure on all social services and employment-generating and poverty-alleviation programmes. The Central Government's per capita real expenditure on the social services more or less paints the same picture.

Taking into consideration the size and severity of poverty in India, unequal access of various socio-economic groups to production resources and the resulting highly unequal distribution of gains of economic growth, the burden of structural adjustment of the Indian economy due to reforms has been mainly falling on the poor. To further worsen the situation, the administrative expenditure incurred in the implementation of the schemes and the pilferages are further reducing the already mimimal effectivenes of these social programmes. On the other hand, unproductive expenditure such as interest payments on the government debt is persistently rising. In all probability, this must be putting an undue burden on the poor.[21]

Thus, Ambedkar's critique of the British Government's expenditure policy of according top priority to unproductive expenditure *vis-à-vis* welfare programmes does appear to hold equally good in the case of post-economic reforms expenditure policy of the government. The government must be also equally

---

21. *Goverment Expenditure on Social Services in Post Reforms period: An Ambedkarian Perspective*, Balchandra Mungekar.

concerned about the situation and taking necessary steps to reverse the trend.

SMALL HOLDINGS IN INDIA AND THEIR REMEDIES

Ambedkar felt that the agricultural farming is by far the most important among the primary industries. India depends almost wholly upon agricultural farming. The problems of agricultural economy dealing directly with agricultural production are what to produce, the proper proportion of the factors of production, the size of holdings, the tenures of land and other related issues. In spite of various reforms ushered in the country, which are implemented in varying degree in different States, agriculture continues to suffer from problems, which Ambedkar envisaged in his Article on "Small Holdings in India and Their Remedies" nearly a century ago. In his Article published in 1918, Ambedkar took on a problem that is still haunting Indian agrarian system of small land-holdings and low-productivity of lands. Ambedkar made a critical examination of the prevailing situation and was of the view that there can be no such thing as a correct size of agricultural holding.[22] As Ambedkar argued, land was only one of the many factors of production and the productivity is one factor of production which is dependent on the proportion in which the other factors of production are combined. In his words: "the chief object of an efficient production consists in making every factor in the concern contribute its highest." He further stated that if agriculture is to be treated as an economic enterprise, there could be no such thing as a large or small holding and certainly it is not due to want of efficiency in utilizing whatever the peasant has, Ambedkar's answer rests on the inadequacy of other factors of production. The

22. Ibid.

insufficiency of capital which is needed for acquiring "agricultural stock and implements" arises from lack of savings. But as Ambedkar remarks: "saving is possible where there is surplus, is a commonplace of political economy."[23] "A large agricultural population with the lowest proportion of land in actual cultivation means that a large part of the agricultural population is superfluous and idle."[24] A consolidated holding should also be an enlarged holding. He advised to keep in mind that the consideration may obviate the evils of scattered holdings, but it would not obviate the evils of holdings unless the consolidated holding is an economic holding, i.e. an enlarged holding. Ambedkar further added even if the lands are consolidated and enlarged and cultivated through capitalistic enterprises, it will not solve the problem as it will only aggravate "the evils by adding to our stock of idle labour." According to Ambedkar, mere holding of land, small or large, does not determine the land to be economic or uneconomic; and the economic holding depends on all the factors of production including land. Consequently, the remedy for the ills of agriculture in India did not lie primarily in the matter of enlarging holdings but in the matter of increasing capital as capital goods. The only way out of this impasse was to take people away from land. This would automatically "lessen and destroy the premimum that at present weighs heavily on land in India and large economic holding will force itself upon us as a pure gain." Ambedkar advised for sponging off this surplus labour for non-agricultural areas to lessen pressure on land. He concludes that "industrialization of India is the soundest remedy for the

23. Babasaheb Ambedkar, *Writings and Speeches*, "Small Holdings in India and Their Remedies", vol. I, Government of Maharashtra, 1979.

24. Ibid.

agricultural sector." Indeed a shift from primary industry to secondary industry is vital and it must be attempted seriously to prevent the present enlargement of the rural population that was being witnessed and remedies based on what he calls "faulty political economy" were being advocated.[25] It is apparent that the rural people still largely depend on agriculture, as industrialization is still lagging behind.

STATE AND MINORITIES

Ambedkar prepared a memorandum "State and Minorities" in 1948 and submitted it to the Constituent Assembly on behalf of All India Scheduled Castes Federation. This memorandum is unique and depicts the blueprint of Ambedkar's model of economic development.

It proposes *state socialism* in important fields of economic life, and it does not leave establishment of state socialism to the will of legislature. It establishes state socialism as the law of the constitution and thus makes it unalterable by any Act of the Legislature and Executive.

SALIENT FEATURES OF SOCIALISM

Some salient features of *state socialism* proposed by Ambedkar are:

1. Key industries shall be owned and run by the state.
2. Industries which are not key industries but are basic shall be owned and run by the state or by corporation established by the State.
3. Insurance shall be the monopoly of the State and the State shall compel every adult citizen to take an insurance policy.
4. Agricultural industry shall be state industry.

25. Ibid.

The scheme shall be brought into operation as early as possible, but in no case shall the period extend beyond the tenth year from the date of the Constitution coming into operations.[26]

Ambedkar had argued for state socialism involving nationalization of agriculture, insurance and basic industries. He desired that there would be neither a land-holder nor a landlord. The objective behind his nationalization policy was to put squarely on the shoulders of the State the duty to supply necessary capital to the industry and agriculture, which would improve the productivity, rapid industrialization and equitable distribution of wealth. He had emphasized nationalization of key and basic industries and agriculture to prevent exploitation of socially and economically deprived classes.

Ambedkar was quite disappointed when his views on collective farming were not accepted. Instead, the Government of India has opted for a more soft measure of land reforms. As the State could not solve the problem of landlessness of SCs in India, the Union Government had opted for redistribution of surplus land in favour of SCs and STs acquired through the implementation of Land Ceiling Act.

The Land and the Scheduled Castes

The SCs and STs even today continue to be poor. The State policy to redistribute surplus land acquired from implementation of Land Ceilings Act has not made substantial progress since there is no surplus acquired land. The fallow lands unoccupied by others were distributed in many states to the SCs. These fallow lands being qualitatively very poor have no access to water supply and also do not have adequate ground water potential.

---

26. Ibid.

Further the employment needs of the landless rural poor, small and marginal farmers are met after 1970s through the implementation of schemes like National Rural Employment Programme (NREP), Integrated Rural Development Programmes (IDRP), etc.

In regard to economy of some socialist countries, the State ownership of industry and agriculture is slowly given to private parties. Ambedkar's economic views, however, should be seen in the context that nearly one-third of population of the country, if not more, still live below poverty line and substantial number of people are landless. The state must, therefore, continue to play a dominant role to bring in economic equality. Ambedkar's economic thought stood for the progressive transformation of society, removing glaring social and economic inequalities.

EXCESSIVE LABOUR IN AGRICULTURE

We are not able to generate any surplus as we are using excessive labour in agriculture. Hence, a large part of agriculture labour was superfluous under the disguise of unemployment. Ambedkar felt that "an idle labour is a calamity and instead of contributing to the national income, it consumes the meagre surplus, which in turn prevents capital formation. Even if we add more capital and capital goods, we will continue to increase the idle labour, as more capital and capital goods, on the given size of the farm does not require much labour force as of now. In the circumstances a part of the agricultural population is superfluous and idle."[27] The economic effects of this idle labour were firstly, it added to

27. *Relevance of Ambedkarism in India*, ed. K.S. Chalam, by G. Nancharaiah, presently Vice-Chancellor, Ambedkar University, Lucknow, Ambedkar on Economic Development. pp. 112-14.

the tremendous amount of pressure of population on land. This enormous pressure was the chief cause of the subdivision of land. When farming was the only occupation the farmers felt that to have a small piece of land was better than having none. This was because of a large population on agriculture to eke out livelihood. Ambedkar felt that it is not the law of inheritance that was the evil, but it was the high pressure of population on land which brings it into operation. People cultivate the small piece of land not because their standard of living was low but because it was the only thing for them to do at present. If they had something more profitable to do, they would never prefer to cultivate the small piece of land. Ambedkar therefore felt "Idle labour therefore, has been the canker of India gnawing at its vitals."[28]

Even if the land holdings were consolidated and enlarged, it would not be a satisfactory solution to our problem in the agricultural sector. If we have succeeded in diverting this idle labour to non-agricultural channels of production, we would at one stroke lessen the pressure on land and destroy the premium that at present weigh heavily on land in India. Besides, this labour when productively employed, would not only earn for his maintenance but would give us surplus and more capital.

His article on "Small Holdings in India and Their Remedies" began with the discussion on small-size holdings, got extended over to the economic analysis of backwardness of the agriculture sector and, as a whole, ended with its solution in the development of the industrial sector. Ambedkar's analysis covered the issue of how to enlarge small and scattered land-holdings and keep them consolidated. The underlying assumption was that fragmented land holdings were too small

28. Ibid. p. 473.

to be economically efficient. He argued that the evil of small land holdings in India was not fundamental but derived from the parent evil of maladjustment in his social economy. Maladjustment resulted mainly on account of distortions in the use of inputs. While capital in the form of capital goods and implements were scarce in relation to land, and agricultural land was scarce in relation to rural population or holdings, the stock of labour force was disproportionately high. The availability of land and capital in relation to each other being limited, this posed major constraints on the optimum use of resource inputs. Ambedkar provided extensive evidence for the decline of average land holdings and the amount of capital goods and implements used in agriculture.

Productivity of agriculture could be increased, according to Ambedkar, by simultaneously expanding capital and capital goods, by reducing labour to raise land and labour productivity and by integrated transfer of labour from agriculture to industry. Ambedkar, therefore, argued for a strategy of transferring labour from agriculture to other sectors of the economy. He advocated that:

> The sponging off of surplus labour in non-agricultural channels of production will at one stroke lessen the pressure and destroy the premium that at present weighs heavily on the land in India. Besides, this labour when productively employed in agriculture and industrial sector will cease to live by predation and will not only earn its keep but will give surplus; and more surplus is more capital. In short, strange that it may seem, industrialization of India is the soundest remedy for the agricultural problems of India.[29]

In short, according to Ambedkar, industrializing India was the surest remedy for her agricultural problems. The

29. Ibid. p. 475.

cumulative effects of industrialization, namely a lessening of pressure on land and increasing amount of capital and capital goods would forcibly create the economic necessity of enlarging the holding. Industrialization is a natural and powerful remedy and is to be preferred.

Ambedkar preferred to cure agriculture by the reflex effects of industrialization. Ambedkar stated that a study was made in the United States in the year 1883 as to how agriculture improves by the reflex effects of industrialization and quoted the summary given by the *London Times* to prove his point:

> The value of farm lands decreases in exact proportion as the ratio of agriculture to other industries increases. That is, where all the labour is devoted to agriculture, the land is worth less than where only half of the people are farm labourers; when only a quarter of them or so are engaged on the farms their products are still more valuable. Manufactures and varied industries thus not only benefit the manufacturers, but are of equal benefit to the farmers as well.[30]

It can be said without fear of challenge that industrialization will foster the enlargement of holdings and that it will be the most effective barrier against sub-division and fragmentation. Industrialization must precede consolidation. Industrialization alone can reduce the extreme pressure that causes sub-division of land. Thus, if small and scattered holdings are the ills from which our agriculture is suffering, industrialization is undeniably the cure.

Revealing his modernistic ideas on industrial capitalistic economy at least on purely economic grounds, Ambedkar stated that "while other countries like the USA starting as agricultural, are progressively becoming industrial, India has

30. Ibid., p. 477.

been gradually undergoing the woeful process of de-urbanization and swelling the volume of her rural population beyond all needs; The earlier we stem this ominous tide, the better." Sir Henry Cotton was quite correct when he said: "There is danger of too much agriculture in India."[31] Not only this, industrialization by cancelling the premium on land would give rise to few occasions for subdividing and fragmenting it.

Ambedkar appeared to have significantly influenced the decision on the strategy of economic planning as well. He emphasized the need for industrialization for overall economic development as well as for development of the agricultural sector. In this sense he laid down a policy framework for general economic development. According to Ambedkar, the poverty in India was due entirely to its dependence upon agriculture alone. Ambedkar argued that:

> India is caught between two sides of pincers, the one side of which is progressive pressure of population and the other is limited availability of land in relation to its needs. The result is that at the end of each decade, we are left with negative balance of population and production and a constant squeezing of standard of living and poverty. The population pressure is giving rise to an army of landless and dispersed families as well. Nothing can open possibilities of making agriculture profitable except a serious drive in favour of industrialization. For it is industrialization alone which can drain away excess of population into gainful employment other than agriculture.[32]

The strategy of economic development enunciated in his paper of 1918 was thus restated twenty-five later in 1943-44, some elements of which were eventually incorporated in the

---

31. Ibid., p. 438.
32. Babasaheb Ambedkar, *Writings and Speeches*, vol. 6, p. 439.

objective of the Reconstruction Plan. This becomes obvious from the following statement of objectives in the Reconstruction Plan paper:

> The ultimate object of all planning must be to raise the standard of living of the people as a whole and ensure employment for all. To that end, the purchasing power of the people must be increased by improvement in the efficiency and consequently the productivity of labour on the one hand; and simultaneous development, and reorganization of agriculture, industries and services on the other.

Agriculture is and will remain India's primary industry but the present imbalanced economy has to be rectified by intensive development of the country's industries so that both agriculture and industry may develop side by side. That will enable the pressure of population on the land to be relieved and will also provide the means required for the provision of better amenities for the people in the way of education, sanitation, public health, housing, etc.[33]

Ambedkar believed in the inter-sectoral transfer of labour from agriculture to industry. In short, he emphasized the need for industrialization of India for overall economic development and industrialization to be the soundest remedy for its agricultural problems. The cumulative effects of industrialization would lead to an increase in labour productivity and capital investment in agriculture. Such transfer of surplus labour from agriculture was expected to increase the productivity and hence the income of the labour remaining in agriculture and also of the labour employed in the industrial sector.

---

33. Ibid., vol. I, p. 477.

Ambedkar preferred fast industrialization in India for many reasons. He maintained that "industrialization facilitates consolidation of land. It lessens the premium of land. It is barrier against future subdivision and consolidation."[34] He was of the opinion that industrialization in India was an absolute necessity. Capital formation through industrialization, to him, was important as it could utilize the surplus labour of countryside for productive purpose. In essence, Ambedkar had visualized what we now refer to as the forward and backward linkages of industrialization.

Ambedkar was aware that the surplus agricultural labour has to be accommodated in industries if we want to solve the problems of unemployement. As such he insisted on capital intensive agriculture as well as industry. The production and employment can be maximized both in agriculture and industry only through increased application of factor inputs like land, labour, capital and machinery for all practical purposes. Ambedkar insisted on considering agriculture as an industry.

AGRICULTURE RURAL DEVELOPMENT

G. Saibaba, in his article on "Dr Ambedkar as a Theoretician and Policy Maker," states:

> Ambedkar's ideas on agricultural development were based on industrial development, institutional reforms which include land reforms and state socialism. As an economist, he predicted and projected the input and output relations that may emerge as a consequence of land reforms. The ills of the Indian agriculture do not lie primarily in the matter of enlarging holdings, but increasing capital and output goods. This implies a production function for the agricultural sector. This idea makes it clear that Ambedkar was keen on treating agriculture as an industry. Thus, he

34. Ibid., p. 478.

> has argued that to step up agricultural output, land reforms should come in a manner that they result in creation of economic holdings. . . His ideas on land reforms were highly practical and original. Ambedkar presented data to show the economic effect of idle labour. Thus, he advocated shifting of this idle labour to non-agricultural activities, where it is productively used. This means that industrialization of India is the soundest remedy for the agricultural problems of India.[35]

As C. Sivarama Krisnarao observes:

> A perspective observation of Ambedkar that had been the hallmark of our development strategy is: "If small and scattered holdings are the ills, from which our agriculture is suffering, to cure it of them is undeniably to industrialise." Hence, Ambedkar's views on small holdings are based on pragmatism and his understanding of the agrarian question and the remedies that he offered are highly relevant to present-day agriculture.[36]

LAND REFORMS

Ambedkar introduced in the Bombay Legislative Council a bill in September 1937 seeking the abolition of the Khoti system. The Khoti system is related to minor land tenures in the Bombay Presidency. It prevailed in some parts of Ratnagiri District and also in some parts of Kolaba (now Raigad) and Thana Districts of Maharashtra. The Khoti tenure differed from the ordinary ryotwari inasmuch as in the latter the occupants of the land were directly responsible to the government for the payments of revenue, while in the former the government employed the services of the Khot for the purpose of collection

35. Ibid., p. 479.
36. G. Saibaba, *Relevance of Ambedkarism in India*, ed. K.S. Chalam, Ambedkar as a Theoretician and Policy Maker, pp. 92-93.

of revenue.[37]

Under the Khoti system the Khot was obliged to collect revenue from the tenants and to pay a certain part of it to the government. Once such payment was made the Khot enjoyed unrestricted freedom to do whatever he liked to the tenants. The Khots generally misused the freedom and subjected the tenants to all kinds of extortions. Thus, by introducing the bill to abolish the Khoti system, Ambedkar sought to put an end to the exploitation of the actual tillers of the land and establish a direct relationship between them and the government. Ambedkar's Bill on the abolition of the Khoti System thus proved to be a forerunner to the Land Reforms Legislation in the post-independent India.[38]

ABOLITION OF WATANS

Ambedkar introduced the Hereditary Office Act Amendment Bill in the Bombay Council in 1928. The intial holders of Watan are government servants according to the Watan Act. These employees are required to work for all the departments of government and at all times, the entire family including the women and children. The government practically pays nothing for their services and they have to depend on the whims and fancies of the farmers for payment of the services rendered by them.[39] *Mahar*[40] got a piece of land or corn from villages.

---

37. Sivaram Krishna Rao, *Relevance of Ambedkarism in India*, ed. K.S. Chalam, Ambedkar's views on Small Holdings in India", p. 121.

38. B.L. Mungekar, *Ambedkar on India's Agrarian Problem*, Reader in Agricultural Economics, Department of Economics, University of Bombay.

39. Babasaheb Ambedkar, *Writings and Speeches*, "Small Holdings and Their Remedies", vol. 2, pp. 99-103.

40. Mahar is a caste in the state of Maharashtra included in Scheduled Caste's list at sl. no. 37.

Ambedkar rightly thought that this had resulted in the loss of self-respect and got it abolished.

Landless Labour

In India, a large chunk of the agricultural labourers come from depressed classes who suffer from social discrimination and economic exploitation. The condition of agricultural labourers was worse particularly before Independence. The problem of the landless labourers was a serious concern for Ambedkar. He propagated the idea that the urgent problem of labourers could be solved by taking over the lands for cultivation and giving them to landless labourers. He emphasized that for the consolidation of holdings the tenancy legislations cannot help Dalits who are landless labourers. He advocated collective farms as they could help them to some extent.

Ambedkar was attracted to the socialism of collective farming. He thought that the State must be owner of the land and distribute the land to all the people, and there should not be any landlords. The collective farming could have helped to solve the basic problems of poverty.

His concept of the society and socialism deserves careful attention — this is aimed at the welfare of the poor classes, ending inequality based on socio-economic factors, maintaining full employment and education, providing social security for the weak and finally rebuilding the Indian society on the foundation of co-operation rather than on rigid social barriers. Ambedkar strongly believed that the fundamental cause of India's backward economy was the delay in changing the land system. The issues raised by Ambedkar for India's socio-economic development are quite pertinent even today. These are related to rural employment, agricultural development, industrial growth, insurance, redistribution of assets, etc. These are contemporary Indian economic problems which

Ambedkar visualized by the mid-twentieth century itself and put forth his views to counter these problems.

Ambedkar's philosophy on collective farming however could not be pursued as it was felt that when minimum needs were met by the State under collective farming, there was no incentive for people to work more and produce more. This view has further been fortified after the collapse of the Communism in Eastern Europe, particularly in former USSR, and these countries have shifted to market-oriented strategies of development.

When we look at Ambedkar's views on land reforms and industrialization not in its isolation but in its integrated form, we gain the impression that Ambedkar was able to visualize, as a true economist, the problems of an economy which was characterized by mass poverty.

The Ninth Five Year Plan (1997-2002), after five decades of planning, continues to accord high priority to agriculture and rural development with a view to generating adequate productive employment and eradication of poverty. The plan also acknowledges that, in our country, the level of agricultural productivity particularly in those areas characterized by poverty is so low that there is sizeable scope and opportunity for increasing agricultural output and thereby increase rural incomes across a wide geographical area.

EMPLOYMENT

It is recognized that the sector which has the greatest employment potential is agriculture. The Ninth Plan goes further and asserts that agricultural growth also has the highest potential for both poverty reduction and correcting regional imbalances. A number of developed and developing countries like Australia, New Zealand, Malaysia and Taiwan, have demonstrated that highly productive agriculture can lead to just as high standards of living as high levels of industrialization with more favourable impact on poverty. It is obvious that we are not able to provide gainful employment to all the rural people. It must also be recognized that modern agriculture is just as much a high technology activity as any industry. Therefore, we should focus our approach on agriculture by imparting appropriate infrastructural training to the farmers including agro-processing. Agriculture provides livelihood for the largest number of our people and robust growth in this sector is the best guarantee of achieving a broad rural areas. Agriculture has not benefited as much as it should have from policies of economic liberalization because agriculture continues to suffer from too many restrictions and impediments which prevent farmers from marketing their produce at remunerative prices.

The agricultural sector has historically played an extremely important role in providing employment in India, and is likely to continue to do so for years to come. The skill profile of the engaging workforce is such that a large majority will have to continue to seek work opportunities in this sector. In order to create such opportunities, land tenancy reforms are essential. Active government intervention, both in implemention of existing laws and formulating new legislation for ensuring the tillers' rights will have to be taken up in earnest in order to create conditions of high labour absorption with adequate a productivity growth. One of the major reasons for India to continue to depend on agriculture for providing employment is that we have failed to industrialize the country in the manner expected to us during the past 50 years, which could have drawn the skilled and semi-skilled workers from the rural areas and reduce their dependence on agriculture.

Given the objectives of removal of the incidence of poverty and unemployment and of ensuring food and nutritional security, attaining a high growth rate in agriculture in the ninth plan and beyond, is necessary. Sustaining an annual rate of 4.5 per cent of agricultural growth would require much larger use of inputs particularly land, irrigation, fertilizers, pesticides, etc. However, the availability of land is expected to emerge as a major constraint on agricultural growth. Due to increasing demand of land for housing in the process of urbanization and industrialization, increasingly larger quantity of agricultural land is being shifted to non-agricultural uses.

It is necessary, as opined by Ambedkar, to improve the standard of living of our poverty-stricken people, apart from seeking necessary measures to improve the productivity in agriculture. There is no alternative but to divert the surplus or unemployed workforce of rural India to gainful employed in medium, large and heavy industries and focus our attention in these areas, if need be, by appropriate incentives. A thorough revamp of controls and the procedures involved at the level of the government would help to create a climate in which Indian agriculture and industry can flourish.

Looked from the present-day point of view, Ambedkar was right in his views on land reforms. Though it has been the declared policy of the Government of India that the land reforms should be recognized to constitute a vital element both in terms of the anti-poverty strategy and for modernization and increased productivity in agriculture, very little has been achieved.

> The full potential of land redistribution has not been realized both in terms of covering the entire surplus that may be available and taken possession of, and for distribution of that already identified. Legal and administrative bottlenecks have led to large gaps between declaration of surplus land, taking actual possession of the

land and its distribution. Appropriate measures have to be taken to reduce the gap.[41]

Industrialization

When Ambedkar assumed the charge as Member, Labour, Irrigation & Power of Executive Council of Viceroy, the problem of reconstruction in India basically was about lack of basic physical infrastructure itself and how to create and develop new infrastucture. Therefore, it was felt that there was a need for long-term plan for building up of basic physical infrastructure in the country, which was the main objective and strategy of the plan. As the development of infrastructure such as electric power, irrigation, communication, road and transport services and technical manpower were treated as prerequisites for industrial development and agriculture, it received top priority in the Reconstruction & Economic Development Plan. It was felt that development of infrastructure would bring a relatively higher growth in industrial output and help to absorb the surplus labour from agriculture. In a policy committee on Public Works and Electric Power, Ambedkar emphasized that the country needed cheap and abundant electricity, without which no effort for industrialization could succeed and development of irrigation and electric power were essential to agricultural productivity.[42]

Ambedkar had very crystal clear and precise perceptions about industrialization.

---

41. Babasaheb Ambedkar, *Writings and Speeches*, vol. 2.
42. *Seventh Five Year Plan*, Planning Commission, Government of India, 1985-90, vol. 11, p. 63.

3

Social Justice

THE Constitution of India, in its quest for social, economic and political justice, offers a special solicitude for hitherto neglected and oppressed segments of the Indian society such as SCs and STs; socially and educationally backward classes; weaker sections of the people and minorities. It also provides mechanisms to ensure protection of their constitutional rights with a view to create an egalitarian social order. It abolishes untouchability and forced labour, and makes discrimination of any kind on the basis of caste, religion or place of birth unconstitutional. These provisions, in ultimate analysis, recognize the right of the depressed classes to be human.

However, one notices a wide gap between the constitutionally, envisaged just and egalitarian social order ensuring socio-economic justice and equality, and visible fraternity, and the actual order in vogue. Vast sections of the SCs and STs are still struggling hard for social justice, which the Preamble to the Constitution pledges to the people of India; while the Fundamental Rights and Directive Principles offer means for its achievement. Notwithstanding the constitutional intent and commitment of social revolution supplemented by appropriate ordinary legislations, the SCs and STs and other weaker sections of the society are still subjected to indignities and inflictive social conditions.

The constitutional commitment of the creation of a classless society befitting equality and human dignity is shattered by the rampant practice of untouchability and labour system. Most inhuman acts originate from caste and economic disparity, particularly in rural India. These two social evils negate the cherished constitutional goals — equality before the law and human dignity.

The constitutional abolition of untouchability and its practice in any form with a view to promoting a new social behaviour has unfortunately not fulfilled the expectations of the framers of the Constitution.[1] The SCs still remain poor, exploited and subjected to social, economic and political disabilities on the ground of untouchability. They have even been denied access to drinking water, a basic human need.[2]

Similarly, despite guaranteeing right against exploitation in the Indian Constitution and abolishing bonded labour system, punishing its practice and providing mechanism for its identification, liberation and rehabilitation by the Bonded Labour System (Abolition) Act, the practice of bonded labour, and other inhuman practices, still exist in India.[3]

Effects of the compensatory discriminatory programmes aimed at social and economic parity between the advanced and backward classes also fail to bring intended result.[4] Distribution of agricultural land to landless persons, another device to ensure socio-economic justice also proved inadequate.[5]

It is important to note that the central government has

1. See generally, Marc Galanter, The Abolition of Untouchability — Missed Opportunities : The use and non-use of Law favourable to untouchables and other specially vulnerable Groups. "*Law and Society in Modern India*, Oxford: 1992, pp. 208-33.
2. Ibid.
3. Ibid.
4. Ibid.
5. Ibid.

officially admitted that despite various measures to improve the social-economic conditions of the SCs and STs, they remain vulnerable and are subjected to various offences, indignities, humiliations, and the disabilities. "Untouchability and the Law," in J. Michael Mahar (ed.), *Untouchability in Contemporary India* (University of Arizona, 1972), pp. 227-14; Desai I.P., *Untouchability in Rural Gujarat* (Popular, 1976); Government of India, *Report of the Committee on Untouchability, Economic and Educational Development of the Scheduled Castes* (1969); Government of India, *Report of the Commissioner for the Scheduled Castes and Scheduled Tribes* (see, successive reports); Upendra Baxi, "The Protection of Civil Right Act; Pitfalls in Implementation," in Upendra Baxi (ed.), *Law and Poverty; Critical Essays* (Tripathi, 1988), pp, 175-85; Parmanand Singh, "The Scheduled Castes and the Law," in Upendra Baxi (ed.), ibid., pp. 132-64; Marc Galanter, "Missed Opportunities: The Use and Non-use of law Favourable to Untouchables and Other Specially Vulnerable Groups," in Marc Galanter, *Law mid society in Modern India* Amid (Oxford, 1992), pp. 208-33; K.I. Vibhute, *Some Problems of Social Disabilities of Scheduled Tribes with Special Reference to Maharashtra*, 4 Ac. L. Rev. 143-60 (1980); Khosta Dinesh, "*Myth and Reality of the Protection of Civil Rights Law : A Case study of Untouchables in Rural India*" (*Hindustan*, Delhi, 1987); Kshirsagar R.K., *Untouchability in Indian Implementation of the Law Abolition* (Deep & Deep, 1986); Pandey Rajendra, *The Caste System in India : Myth and Reality* (Criterion, New Delhi, 1986); Ainapur, *Dynamics of Caste Relations in Rural India* (Rawart, Jaipur, 1986), and Praful Bidwai, "Abolishing Untouchability: Biggest Hurdle is Hindu Communalism," *The Times of India*, Bombay, 2 February 1992.

It has been empirically shown that 67 per cent of Gujarat village untouchables were denied access to wells (see, I.P. Desai, ibid.). A survey conducted by the All India Harijan Sevak Sangh in 1155 villages from 12 States has revealed that in all the villages surveyed in Karnataka and Orissa the SCs were denied access to wells. Situation in Himachal Pradesh, Rajasthan, Uttar Pradesh and Gujarat was also found equally appalling (see, Government of India, *Report of the Commissioner for the Scheduled Castes and Scheduled Tribes (1978-79)*. pp. 182-87). Similarly, a recent extensive survey conducted in 95 villages of four districts of Marathwada region (Maharashtra) by the Vidhayak Sansad Vasi, reveals that in more than half of the villages common drinking water facility was not available. (*The Times of India*, Bombay, 3 September 1991). Also see Upendra Baxi, "Righting Ancient Wrongs," *Indian Express*, Bombay, 14 March 1993.

Generally see K.C. Alexander, *Abolition of Bonded Labour* (National Institute of Community Development, Hyderabad, 1976); Anand Dubey, *Social Justice and Bonded Labour Force in India* (Printwell Pub., Jaipur, 1989); Bharati Dogra, *Bonded Labour : Myth and Yojana*, May 1-15 (1987), p. 29 and R.K. Tiwari *Enforcement of Bonded Labour System Abolition Act : A Review, Jr. of Social Economic Studies* (1985) no. 4, p. 2. It is worth noting that 2,42,618 bonded labourers were identified, as on 31 March 1989 (vide Lal Bahadur Shastri National Academy of Administration, Mussoorie. *Study Report on Bonded Labour*, 1990), and only 11,344 cases have been registered against the bonded labour keepers out of a total number of 2 lakh bonded labour keepers (vide, Government of India, *Report by the Ministry of Labour*, March, 1990).

Generally see, Marc Gulanter, *Combating Equalities Law and the Backward Classes in India* (Oxford, 1984); Parmanand Singh, *Equality, Reservation and Discrimination in India : A Constitutional Study of Scheduled Caste and Scheduled Tribes and Other Backward Classes* (Deep & Deep 1982); Government of India, *Report of the Backward Classes Commission* (1955) and Government of India, *Report of the Backward Classes Commission* (1981).

See K.I. Vibhuta, "Socio-Economic Justice Through Land Distribution," C.J. Samuel et al. (ed.), *Principles of Legislation and Judicial Process* (University of Poona 1992) pp. 274; K. Gopal Iyer, *Report on the Empirical Study of Land Reforms in India*, Vol. 1-5 (Lal Bahadur Shastri National Academy of Administration, Mussoorie, 1990) and Government of India, *Report of the Committee to Study the Progress of Mechanism for Land Allotment to the Scheduled Castes and their Representation in Services* (1967).

It is significant to note that Article 31B inserted by the Constitution (First Amendment) Act 1951, protects land reform legislations and agrarian laws enumerated in the Ninth Schedule from challenge in any court of law on the ground that such a legislation (or regulation or provision thereof) is inconsistent with, or takes away or abridges, any of the Fundamental Rights guaranteed in Part III of the Constitution. The amendment facilitates creation of a just society by enabling the States to achieve smooth distribution of agricultural land to landless persons and protect them from harassment.[6]

However, it is a matter of common knowledge that when measures employed in pursuance of the constitutional commitment to, and promise of, social revolution, and of the statutes enacted or schemes formulated in pursuance of the constitutional mandate, giving preferential treatment — social, economic and political — to the depressed segments of the society and intending removal of their social and economic disabilities, (such as abolition of untouchability and bonded-labour, reservation of seats in employment and professional courses, distribution of land and allotment of house sites, etc.) are implemented. When potential beneficiaries of such

6. See, Statement of Objects and Reasons of the Scheduled Castes and Scheduled Tribes (Prevention of Atrocities), Bill, 1989, Gazette of India, dated 7 August 1989, Ext. Sec. 2, p. 11.

measures have asserted what is "just and theirs," the advanced section of the society, whose vested interests are at stake, because of implementation of these measures, has violently reacted at the slightest possible excuse.[7] The Central Government while moving the Scheduled Castes & Scheduled Tribes (Prevention of Atrocities) Bill of 1989, had to admit the fact of increasing incidents of atrocities on and harassment of the SCs and STs as a sequel to the preferential treatment given to them by the State. The renaming of the Marathwada University, Aurangabad after the late Ambedkar caused the Dalits damage to the tune of Rs. 17,49,331. 1065 huts of Dalits were damaged in 73 villages whereby 6370 Harijans were affected. Two dalits lost their lives (see, Shroff, "Why Marathwada University Alone" (Jaihind Press, Aurangabad, 1978); *The Times of India*, Bombay, 7 August 1978 and 20 August 1978; also see, Chichunsure B. Rights, *Social Equality and Riots : A Study with Reference to Recent Riots in Marathwada* (1980). Recently 12 Dalits were attacked in Aurangabad district of Marathwada for the fourth time by upper-caste Hindus with the intention of driving them away from grazing land which they had been cultivating for several years (see, *The Times of India*, Bombay, 25 September 1992). In March 1993 three Harijans were killed in Mysore district who sought entry into a temple through a court order (see, *The Times of India*, 18 April 1993). The officially admitted number of incidents of atrocities against the SCs and STs till 1992 are 18,014. (see *The Times of India*, Bombay, 24 May 1993, also see, N.D. Kamble *Atrocities on Scheduled Castes in Independent India* (Institute of Social and Economic Change, Hyderabad, 1979).

Because of the awareness created amongst the SCs and STs through spread of education, etc. they are trying to assert their rights and this is not being taken very kindly by the

7. For example, during the 1978 controversy over the

others. When they assert their rights and resist the practice of untouchability or demand statutory minimum wages or refuse to do any bonded and forced labour, the vested interests try to cow them down and terrorize them. Occupation and cultivation of even the government-allotted land to them is resented and more often these people become victims of attacks by vested interests.[8]

Attempts at reconstruction of a new social order in India on the modern foundations of justice and equality have thus been receiving serious setbacks and there have been severe jerks owing to the increasing instances of atrocities on the proposed beneficiaries from such schemes. As such, special courts have been set up for the trial of offences against the SCs and STs as well as for providing relief and rehabilitation to the victims of such offences. However, its effect is yet to be realized.

According to the National Commission for the Scheduled Castes and Scheduled Tribes, 4022 SCs/STs were murdered and 1,15,055 crimes against Dalits were reported between 1981 and 1986. Among the reasons cited by the Commission for this violence are: land disputes, alienation of tribal land, bonded labour, indebtedness, wage disputes and casteism. See, Government of India, *Report of the National Commission for the Scheduled Castes and Scheduled Tribes* (1990). Also see, Government of India, *Report of the Commissioner for the Scheduled Castes and Scheduled Tribes (Twenty-fifth Report, 1986-87)*, p. 228.

Thus, the existing social order unequivocally demonstrates a wide gap between the constitutionally promised egalitarian

8. Supra No. 59 at p. 11.

In 1989 Parliament enacted the Scheduled Castes and Scheduled Tribes (Prevention of Atrocities) Act, 1989 to prevent the commission of atrocities against the SCs and STs.

social order and its actual performance. Little is done, vast is undone in pursuance of the constitutional scheme and spirit. A serious and comprehensive review of pertinent factors — social, political, economic and legal — thwarting the attainment of the constitutional goals, therefore, becomes imperative. Otherwise it will cause threat not only to the social order but also to the social order envisaged by the founding fathers of the Indian Constitution.

Ambedkar, the principal architect of the Constitution who personally experienced the anomalous ill-effects of the centuries-old socio-economic inequalities and indignities and who came to the Constituent Assembly to ameliorate the plight of the SCs and STs, lamented:

> Political democracy cannot last unless there lies at the base of it social democracy. What does social democracy mean? It means a way of life which recognizes liberty, equality and fraternity. They are not to be treated as separate items in a trinity. They form a union of trinity in the sense that to divorce one from the other is to defeat the very purpose of democracy. Liberty cannot be divorced from equality, equality cannot be divorced from liberty. Nor can liberty and equality be divorced from fraternity. Without equality, liberty would produce the supremacy of the few over the many. Equality without liberty would kill individual initiative. Without fraternity, liberty and equality could not become a natural course of things. We must begin by acknowledging the fact that there is a complete absence of two things in Indian society based on the principle of graded inequality which means elevation for some and degradation for others. On the economic plane, we have a society in which there are some who have immense wealth as against many who live in abject poverty.[9]

---

9. *Constituent Assembly Debates*, vol. 11, pp. 944-45.

He questioned:

> How long shall we continue to live this life of contradictions? How long shall we continue to deny equality in our social and economic life?[10]

And he apprehended:

> If we continue to deny it for long, we will do so only by putting our political democracy in peril. We must remove this contradictions at the earliest possible moment or else those who suffer from inequality will blow up the structure of political democracy which this Assembly has so laboriously built up.[11]

It is, therefore high time to review and re-examine, at least in the centenary year of Bharat Ratna Ambedkar, which is being observed as Social Justice Year by the Government of India, the factors hampering the attainment of the constitutional goal of an egalitarian social order with a view to renewing sincere and honest efforts on the part of the "policy makers" and "policy implementers" to turn Ambedkar's dream into reality. It undoubtedly needs strong political will and courage to relentlessly, honestly and effectively implement the constitutional mandate and to honour the constitutional spirit by rising above petty party politics, politics of caste and politics of reservation.[12]

Ambedkar's Contribution to Social Justice

Every society, from time immemorial, has been making its best efforts to ensure happiness and peace to its members by guaranteeing fulfilment of their needs, alleviating their

10. Ibid.
11. Ibid.
12. K.I. Vibhute, "Ambedkar's Sense of Social Justice and Constitutional Spirit", *Mainstream*, vol. 31, no. 22, 10 April 1993, p. 25.

sorrows and sufferings, protecting them from abuse and exploitation, i.e. by doing justice. Before making any attempt to understand social justice, it becomes essential to clarify the concept of justice *per se*. Miller (1967 : 17) has aptly remarked:

> The concept of social justice is best understood as forming one part of the broader concept of justice in general. To comprehend it properly, we should begin by looking at justice as a whole, and then attempt to mark off that division of justice which we call social justice.

The term justice has a very vast canvas and it is very difficult to give a very precise but comprehensive definition. Dias (1985 : 65-66) has rightly observed: "The concept of justice is too vast to be encompassed by one mind."

Justice is not something which can be captured in a formula once and for all; it is a process, a complex and shifting balance between many factors. Krishnamurthy (1982 : 18) has also maintained that "in spite of best efforts, it has not been possible to clearly define justice." However, attempts have been made from time to time to define justice. Traditionally, justice means "the virtue by which we give to every man what is his due, opposed to injury or wrong." Today, justice means protection of legal rights. The tasks of justice are "the just allocation of advantages and disadvantages, preventing the abuse of power, preventing the abuse of liberty, the just decision of disputes and adapting the change" (Dias, 1985 : 66). The Justice may be natural or distributive or corrective in nature. The Natural Justice refers to the rules and procedures to be followed by a person or body with the duty of adjudicating upon disputes between the rights of others, e.g. rules requiring such person to act fairly, in good faith, without bias in a judicial temper after providing opportunity to be heard (Desai, 1983 : 1590).

Distributive Justice is based on the principle of equality whereas *Corrective Justice* seeks to restore equality where it has been disbursed because of some kind of wrongdoing.

Social Justice as a form of justice means what is socially just and varies with time and space. Alien (1950 : 31) has rightly pointed out:

> We hear much today of social justice. I am not sure that those who use the term most glibly know very clearly what they mean by it. Some mean "distribution" or "redistribution" of wealth, some interpret it as *equality of opportunity* — a misleading term since opportunity can never be equal among human beings who have unequal capacities to grasp it; many, I suspect, mean simply that it is unjust that anybody be more fortunate than themselves, and more intelligent, and mean that it is just — I would rather say benevolent — that every effort should be made at least to mitigate the disparities of human inequality and that no obstacle should be offered, but rather help afforded, to provide practicable opportunities for self-improvement.

Social justice is a dynamic term which provides sustenance to the "rule of law." It helps in the establishment of a just structure by removing social and economic inequality with the help of law on the one hand, and ensures freedom for optimal personality development of the individual on the other; of course with a tilt in favour of removal of structural inequalities, equalization by providing special opportunities to the weaker and vulnerable sections of society. The main objective of social justice is to remove man-made inequalities — political, economic and social — particularly by guaranteeing equal opportunities to all citizens in various types of political, economic and social activities.

Pettit (1980 : IX) has explored:

> the three accounts of social justice which have dominated the recent debate. They are: the proprietarian account, which makes natural rights the last court of appeal in political

> assessment; the utilitarian, which looks to human happiness in the judgement of rival social schemes; and the contractarian, an approach which identifies the just arrangement as that which people would have reason to choose were they ignorant of how they would fare under the different alternatives. The first assimilates justice to legitimacy, the second to welfare, and the third to fairness.

A probe into the basic tenets of these three accounts unravels three criteria: (1) to each according to his right; (2) to each according to his desire; and (3) to each according to his need. In developing countries like India with welfare orientation of States and with vast social, economic and political inequalities resulting from basically inegalitarian social structure, minimum needs of people will have to be satisfied and opportunities for fullest development to everyone will have to be given, particularly by adopting special measures for protecting and promoting interests of the weaker and vulnerable sections.

Ambedkar's contribution to social justice is being analysed here in four categories: (1) Contribution to emancipation and development of SCs; (2) Promotion of interest of minorities; (3) Improvement of position of women; and (4) Betterment in the conditions of labour.

CONTRIBUTION TO EMANCIPATION AND DEVELOPMENT OF SCs

Ambedkar was against the social system of Brahmanical Hindus. According to him, the main principles of Brahmanism are:

(i) graded inequality between the different classes;

(ii) complete, disarmament of the shudras and the untouchables;

(iii) complete prohibition of education of the shudras and the untouchables;

(iv) ban on the shudras and the untouchables occupying places of power and authority (Ahluwalia and Ahluwalia, 1981 : 88). He suggested following changes in the Hindu outlook:

(1.) There should be one and only one standard work of Hindu Religion acceptable to all Hindus and recognized by all Hindus.

(2.) Priesthood among Hindus should be abolished.

(3.) No ceremony should be allowed to be performed by a priest who does not hold a legally valid *sanad.*

(4.) Priests should be servants of the state and should be subject to disciplinary action; and

(5.) The number of priests should be legally limited according to the requirements of the state (cited in Lokhande, 1982 : 130-31).

Ambedkar considered the castes as enclosed units. According to him,

castes are enclosed units and it is their conspiracy with clear conscience that compels the ex-communicated to make themselves into a caste. The logic of this adverse circumstance is merciless, and it is in obedience to its force that some unfortunate groups find themselves enclosed, because others in enclosing themselves have closed them out with the result new groups. . . by a mechanical law are constantly being converted into castes with a bewildering multiplicity (Ambedkar, 1917 : 81-85).

He was of the view that caste system is the root of untouchability. He maintained:

> The root of untouchability is the caste system, the root of the system is caste attached to varnashrama: and the root of varnashrama is the Brahmanical religion and the root of Brahmanical religion is authorization of political power.
>
> — cited in Prakash, 1993 : 52

In Ambedkar's opinion:

> (1) the shudras were one of the Aryan communities of the solar race; (2) the shudras ranked as kshatriya varna in the Hindu Aryan society; (3) there was a time when the Aryan society recognized only three varnas; namely brahmins, kshatriyas, and vaishyas. The shudras were not a separate varna but a part of the kshatriya varna; (4) there was a continuous feud between the shudra kings and the brahmins in which the brahmins were subjected to many tyrannies and indignities; (5) as a result of the hatred towards the shudras due to their tyrannies and oppressions, the brahmins refused to invest the shudras with the sacred thread; and (6) owing to the loss of the sacred thread, the shudras became socially degraded, fell below the rank of *vaishyas* and came to form the fourth *varna*.
>
> — Ambedkar, 1947 : 239

Ambedkar was of the view that the shudras in Hindu *varna* system were worse than slaves. He clearly wrote:

> In slavery the master at any rate had the responsibility to feed, clothe and house the slave and keep him in good condition lest the market value of the slave should decrease. But in the system of untouchability, the Hindu takes no responsibility for the maintenance of the untouchable. As in any economic system, it permits exploitation without obligation. Untouchability is not only a system of unmitigated economic exploitation but it is also a system of uncontroller economic to condemn it and there is no impartial machinery of administration to restraint it. There is no appeal to public opinion, for, whatever public opinion there is, it is the opinion of the Hindus who belong to the exploiting class and as such favour exploitation. There is no check from the police or the judiciary for the simple reason that they are all drawn from the Hindus and take the side of the exploiters. — cited in Lokhande, 1982 : 30

He was strongly opposed to Brahmanical Hindu social order and exhorted the shudras to adopt any religion other than Hinduism. At the end of his life, he himself got initiated into Buddhism.

For the removal of untouchability, Ambedkar wanted that the concept of socio-religious or ritual status should be replaced by the secular status based on the principle of one man, one value; one man, one vote. Ambedkar launched a crusade against untouchability by creating public opinion through his writings in several periodicals like *Mook Nayak, Bahishkrit Bharat, Equality, Janata,* etc. started by him; and by organizing protest marches like the renowned Mahad march for entitling the shudras to draw water from the famous Chavdar tank, and the Nasik Satyagrah for permitting entry of the untouchables into the Kala Ram temple. He believed that the problem of emancipation of the shudras was basically a problem of political, economic and social equality. He maintained: "there can be no gainsaying as political power in this country has too long been a monopoly of a few, and that many are not only beasts of burden but also beasts of prey. This monopoly has not merely deprived them of their chance of betterment, it has snapped them of what may be called the significance of life. These downtrodden people are tired of being governed. They are impatient to govern themselves. The urge for self-realization in the downtrodden classes must not be allowed to devolve into a struggle or class war. . . . This can only be done by the establishment of equality and fraternity in all walks of life" (cited in Rajasekhariah, 1989 : 225).

Here political equality was not enough for the emancipation of the shudras; what is really required is equality in social and economic life. Participating in the Constituent Assembly debate, he declared without mincing words:

> . . . on the 26th January, 1950, we are going to enter into a life of contradictions. In politics we will have equality; and in social and economic structure, we continue to deny the principle of one man, one value. How long shall we we continue to deny equality in our social and economic life? If we continue to deny it for long, we will do so only by putting our political democracy in peril. We must remove this contradiction at the earliest possible moment or else those who suffer from inequality will blow up the structure of political democracy. — Cited in Rajasekhariah, 1989 : 224

Ambedkar wanted social justice to be ensured by making provisions in this regard in the Constitution itself. In the memorandum — A Scheme of Political Safeguards for the Depressed Classes in the Future Constitutions of India — submitted to the First Round Table Conference, he laid down model articles on Fundamental Rights. Various political safeguards envisaged by Ambedkar for the Depressed Classes and submitted to the Round Table Conference included: (1) equal citizenship and fundamental rights declaring the practice of untouchability as illegal; (2) free enjoyment of equal rights protected by Constitutional remedies; (3) protection against discrimination; (4) adequate representation to the Depressed Classes in the legislatures; adult suffrage and separate electorates to the Depressed Classes for 10 years; (5) adequate representation in services; (6) redress against prejudicial action or neglect or interest, facilities for education, etc.; (7) Special departmental care, special minister and welfare bureaus; and (8) seat in the cabinet. (Ahluwalia and Ahluwalia, 1981 : 95).

For politicial emancipation of the shudras, Ambedkar wanted reservation in Legislature; for economic development he desired discontinuance of untouchability; for social rehabilitation he advocated intercaste dining and marriage and even change of Hindu religion. He himself started People's Education Society in 1946 which established Siddhartha Groups of Educational Institutions in Bombay and Milind Group of Institutions in Aurangabad. Ambedkar wanted the shudras to believe in self-help and organized themselves to achieve their rights. He has very clearly pointed out: "my heart breaks to see the pitiable plight of your faces and to hear your sad voices. You have been groaning from time immemorial and yet you are not ashamed to hug your helplessness as an inevitability. You had better died and relieve this world if you could not rise to a new life and if you could not rejuvenate yourself. As a matter of fact it is your birthright to get food, shelter and clothing . . . if you believe in living a respectable life, you should believe in self-help which is the best help.(cited in Lokhande, 1982 : 17).

He made a clarion call to the shudras not to be satisfied and self-complacent and to cherish the belief that man is the creator of history and he will come out successful, notwithstanding the odd circumstances. He always advocated establishment of organizations for the uplift of SCs and himself started organizations like Depressed Classes League, Bahiskrit Sabha, Buddhist Society of India, Bhartiya Bahiskrit Samaj Sevak Sangh, Samta Mandal, Samta Sainik Dal, Mahar Watandar Gavkamgar Association and even formed Independent Labour Party and later on Republican Party of India. He saw a threat to the untouchables from dominant agricultural castes in the democratic set-up. He gave the slogan: "to live with respect is a birthright of man."

PROMOTION OF INTERESTS OF MINORITIES

Ambedkar had a special concern for the development of minorities. During the British regime, he vehemently fought for their rights. His views on the minority problems were concretely expressed in the Memoranda submitted by him to the Simon Commission and at the round Table Conferences. As a member of the Minorities Committee, Ambedkar supported the demands made by the minorities for proper representation in the Legislature, the Executive and the Public Services as also for the statutory prevention of discrimination of the minorities by the majority. He was convinced that national well-being and liberty would depend upon the rights enjoyed by the minorities. He always entertained a fear that majority with its orthodox Hindu beliefs and prejudices could easily violate the dictates of justice, equality and good conscience, and the minorities might be discriminated against in several ways. He favoured special consideration for the minority communities because it is "weak either in numbers or because its social standing is low or its educational standing is backward as compared with others or because its economic strength is not sufficient to place it on a fighting level with other communities." (cited in Rajasekhariah, 1989 : 92). Ambedkar always placed a special responsibility on the majority community to allay the fears of the minorities. He has clearly stated that: "the majority community must see to it that all fears of minorities are set at rest" (cited in Rajasekhariah, 1989 : 93).

Ambedkar had worked out the details of a safe polity for minorities and prepared a "ground plan" under which special protection was required to be given to all minorities in general and the SCs in particular who were more in need of protection than the religious minorities in the country.

IMPROVEMENT OF POSITION OF WOMEN

Ambedkar was fully familiar with the pitable situation of women in the Hindu society for which he wanted radical changes in the Hindu family in particular and Hindu society in general. With regard to the Hindu family, he wanted solution of the problems of *sati*, widow remarriage, child marriage, etc. whereas in respect of the Hindu society he desired abolition of caste system and untouchability and amendment in the laws relating to marriage, adoption, succession, etc. He went to the extent of burning a copy of *Manusmriti* when he advocated discrimination on the basis of caste and sex. He prepared a Hindu Code Bill incorporating matters relating to: (1) right of property of a deceased Hindu who has died intestate, i.e. without making a will, to both female and male; (2) the order of succession among the different heirs to the property of a deceased dying intestate; (3) the law of maintenance; (4) marriage; (5) divorce; (6) adoption; and (7) minority and guardianship (Ambedkar, 1949 : 12-37). Though the Bill could not be passed and Ambedkar had to resign from the post of Law Minister, a firm ground was laid for the enactment of the Hindu Marriage Act, the Hindu Succession Act, the Hindu Adoption and Maintenance Act and the Hindu Minority and Guardianship Act which have since significantly improved the position of women in the Hindu society.

Ambedkar made a multi-dimensional contribution to the empowerment of women in India by advocating girls' education, removal of social attitudes in treating women, maternity benefits for working women during the period of pregnancy and the right to separation, divorce maintenance, adoption and succession. Ambedkar always held the view that the progress of any society can be estimated on the basis of advancement of women in that society.

Ambedkar advised women in India to live hygienically, to remain away from all evils, to educate their children, to safeguard their children against developing any kind of inferiority complex, to make their children ambitious, and not to marriage them off in haste or in a hurry.

Ambedkar wanted women to be bold and fearless like

men. Citing examples from history, he averred that the women of this country had always proved that they not only could work within the four walls of their houses but could also fight on the war front. He used to advise SC women not to consider themselves as untouchables or inferior but to live a pure and clean life and to wear clothes like cultured women, and not mind their clothes having patches or being dressed in totters. He however exhorted them to wear clean clothes.

Ambedkar considered education for women to be as essential as for men because children usually emulate both their parents. He advised women to so mould their children that they would lead a life of virtue.

BETTERMENT IN THE CONDITION OF LABOUR

Ambedkar formed an Independent Labour Party in 1936 at the time of elections to the Bombay Assembly. He organized a strike to end the exploitation and repression of mill workers of Bombay but because the strike was declared illegal by the State Govenment he dissociated himself from the Congress ministry constituted on 19 July 1937 and continued with his struggle. He was included in the Executive Council of the Viceroy as a Labour Member on 2 July 1943.

While presiding over a meeting of Standing Labour Committee constituted by the Indian Labour Conference, he gave a call for the constitution of Joint Labour Committee. He stressed the need for the establishment of Employment Exchanges for helping the unemployed in finding employment.

While presiding over the second Indian Labour Conference in Delhi, he stressed the need for evolving some arrangement to consider the question of wages and income and social security for workers. In April 1944, he presented an amendment bill providing for leave with wages to workers for continuous period or workers in factories.

Ambedkar was convinced of the utility of compulsory arbitration and wanted to make it a part of permanent Labour Code.

While presiding over the seventh Session of Indian Labour Conference on 27 November 1945, Ambedkar exhorted workers to ask the owners of their factories as to why they failed to spend money on the upgradation of their standards.

While presiding over a meeting of Regional Labour Commissioners in Delhi, Ambedkar stressed the need for strengthening the conciliation machinery and making the necessary amendment in the Minimum Wages Act. He firmly held the view that tripartism was the only way to permanent peace. He solemnly averred that by putting an end to exploitation, organizing welfare measures and promoting proper industrial relations, industrial peace could be brought about.

Ambedkar was seriously concerned about the problem of landless labourers which he thought was the outcome of the typical agricultural situation, and more than that, the result of the peculiar Indian economy. Ambedkar as a sensitive enlightened and vigilant social thinker was concerned about the development of all kinds of weaker and vulnerable sections of Indian society and fought for their betterment by awakening and organizing them and by exerting pressure on the government to enact laws to ensure social justice to them always bearing in mind that the law was the most potent tool of social transformation. And it goes to the credit of Ambedkar that several provisions for the protection of the interests of the SCs, STs, minorities, labour, and women belonging to the weaker and vulnerable sections of the society have been made in the Constitution of India for which his name will go down in the annals of India.

4

Mandal Commission and Judicial Responses

TILL the framing of the Constitution of India the Indian National Congress never took a firm stand over the removal of untouchability. It, in its annual session at Calcutta in 1917, passed a vague resolution in this regard. The focus of the resolution was on bringing social justice to the depressed classes and on removing their disabilities forced by age-old customs. The Indian National Congress decided that it should not deflect from its main objective of winning freedom. It feared that attention to reforms would have a harmful effect on the national struggle. In 1895, its tone became sympathetic to social reforms.

The Indian National Congress split up into two camps — one professing social reforms and the other advocating exclusion of social reforms from its programme. These happenings unfolded a trend in the Indian National Congress, and Dr Ambedkar considered it to be a political gain — the Indian National Congress was trying to seek the support of the depressed classes in return for recognition of their demands. The Indian National Congress Committee ridiculously handed over the task of removing untouchability to the Hindu Mahasabha in May 1923. The problems of the untouchables engaged significant attention at the time of the holding of the First Round Table Conference (1930). Two representatives of the untouchables were invited and this recognized the fact that the interests of the untouchables were different from those of the caste Hindus. The first Round Table Conference was presented a memorandum by Ambedkar which covered adequate representation of the depressed classes in Legislature, measures against boycott or threat of boycott, protection against discrimination, adequate reservation in services, right to redressal against prejudiced action, or neglecting their interests, formation of a special department for taking up cases of untouchables and their representation in the cabinet.

The Minorities Committee agreed to award separate electorates to the depressed classes. It was also made clear that the minorities should be represented in the provincial and federal executives. If a small minority did not get representation in the cabinet, a minister specially charged with the duty of safeguarding their interests was to be appointed. The committee pointed out that the minorities and depressed classes were free to refuse their consent to any Constitution which could not safeguard their interests. Mahatma Gandhi was chosen to represent the cabinet; he resisted special representation to the untouchables after a compromise between the Congress and British Government. Ambedkar was annoyed by the reference made by Gandhiji to the effect that the representatives of minority communities were not elected, but they were merely nominees of British Government. Ambedkar feared that power was likely to be transferred to the high castes by the British Government.

Gandhiji did not take a firm stand on the question of untouchables. The upper caste Hindus particularly brahmins were occupying important positions in the ministry and administrative services. The interests of the depressed classes were not safe in the hands of the Congress and its leaders.

Here, it was necessary to embody certain safeguards for them in the Constitution itself. Ambedkar constantly fought for Constitutional safeguards for the depressed classes.

The problem was not to be solved by showing lip sympathy to the depressed classes. Certain attempts were made to assimilate, but according to Ambedkar separatism existed in Hinduism as the upper caste Hindus never liked untouchables to claim their material share. Up to the arrival of the British Government in India, the untouchables were dormant politically, economically and socially. However, with the idea of equality before law brought forth by the Britishers, a new era started for them. The state took quite a philanthropic attitude towards the untouchables. Efforts were made to abolish untouchability. Ambedkar for the first time demanded liberties for the untouchables. He encountered confrontation with a top-ranking leader like Mahatma Gandhi.

Dr Babasaheb Ambedkar put pressure on the caste Hindus to bury age-old traditions founded on inequality. Gandhiji did not welcome Ambedkar's idea because they were revolutionary and attacked the foundation of Hinduism. Since he confined himself to the uplift of the untouchables only, he could mobilize them with greater case. The social and political activities of Ambedkar had considerable impact on the ideology and programmes of the Congress and Gandhiji. They had to turn their attention to attempts at removing untouchability. As events drifted the Congress in course of time sought the help of Ambedkar.

In order to settle the communal problem the Nehru Committee was appointed under the chairmanship of Motilal Nehru. The Committee assured all non-Hindu and linguistic minorities of security and protection. The recommendations of the Nehru Report gave fundamental rights to all citizens, and guaranteed religious liberty which the minorities were worried about. Disapproving separate electorates, it recommended joint ones with reservation for the Muslims.

Dr Babasaheb Ambedkar was shown a token honour by being made the Chairman of the Constitution Draft Committee. The objectives resolution put forward by Pandit Nehru, which later on formed the text of the preamble, guaranteed justice as regards economic, political, social fields and safeguards for the SCs, STs and Other Backward Classes (OBCs) in India.

Dr Babasaheb Ambedkar submitted a memorandum in which he asserted that political and economic safeguards for the SCs and STs should be guaranteed in the Constitution and their representation to be made on the basis of their population. He preferred separate electorates for the untouchables. The Sub-committee on Minorities submitted its report to the Advisory Committee which accepted its recommendations. Further, the Advisory Committee forwarded its report to the President of the Constituent Assembly. Reservation of seats for the Christians, Muslims and the SCs was accepted. The members of the minorities were allowed to contest unreserved seats also. But as far as the seats in the cabinet were concerned, there was no reservation. Article 299(1) of the draft Constitution laid down the provision of a special officer who was given the right to enquire into all matters concerning privileges to the minorities. Further, according to Articles 300 and 301, a commission was to be appointed for investigating the problems pertaining to the OBCs.

Article 14 abolished the existing injustice to the STs. It further implied removal of discrimination on the basis of caste, sex, sect, etc., and free access by all citizens of India to public places, shops, hotels and places of entertainment was ensured. The use of public wells, roads, bathing ghats, tanks, etc. was thrown open to all. This provision, in the Constitution, is really revolutionary.

Article 16 gives an assurance of equality of opportunity in public employment. According to Article 16(4) the State will not be prevented from making any provision for the reservation of appointment in favour of any backward class of citizens, which in the opinion of the State is not adequately represented in the services under the State. Ambedkar placed considerable emphasis on creating an educated middle class which might have great potential for exacting social reforms.

The Constitution makes an earnest attempt at removing untouchability. Article 17 of the Constitution provides that untouchability stands removed, and its practice in any shape or form has been made a punishable offence. An attempt has been made to trace out the efforts made by the Indian National Congress and Ambedkar to abolish untouchability. No doubt, the growth of the Indian democratic system was to rest on the principle of equality. The principle is artistically fused with Articles 14, 15, 16, 29(2), 44, 325 and 326.

The clauses relating to equality have special reference to backward classes. Dr Babasaheb Ambedkar said that political democracy could not survive in the absence of social democracy. In his opinion social democracy assures and implements liberty, equality and fraternity as principles of life. Ambedkar advised the SCs to safeguard their privileges. It is their right to refuse any change if they felt no guarantee was given to safeguard their rights.[1]

Dr Babasaheb Ambedkar's constant pressure on the Congress including Gandhiji moulded the Constitution. Article 335 was the total effect of the process. The Commissioner for

---

1. Keer, Dr Ambedkar: *Life and Mission*, 2nd edn., 1991, p. 412.

Schedule Castes and Scheduled Tribes explained that Article 335 is mandatory because the language used in almost all the articles is the same. The backward classes had no adequate representation, nor had they got an opportunity to an adequate share in the services. No uniform criterion was used in fixing up "quota" for which reservation should be continued. This shows that the framers of the Constitution left these things to the conscience of the government. The population of the SCs and STs was not evenly distributed, so fixing the quota uniformly would not have been proper.

Kakasaheb Kalelkar a prominent leader was appointed chairman of Backward Classes Commission (29 January 1953). Eleven members including the Chairman constituted the Commission. Kalelkar said that he was definitely against reservation in government service for any community since the services are meant for the society as a whole. The best policy that could be recommended was that given the same or almost the same qualifications, candidates or aspirants from the backward classes should be given a decided preference.[2]

The Commission gave thought to the possible means for identifying socially and educationally backward classes other than the SCs and STs. It identified backward classes on basis of their poverty, backwardness in education, lack of means of communication due to their being in interior areas, state and extent of unemployment and existence of defective education having no link with practical matters. The commission did not hesitate to accept caste as a basis of backwardness.[3]

The Constitutional issue of reservation apart from being related to the standard of administration is also related to the

2. *Report of the Backward Classes Commission*, vol. I, p. 8.
3. Ibid., p. 55.

concept of social justice which is fused with so many clauses in the Indian Constitution.

India has a long history of caste-ridden society. The social relations have always been based on caste identification. Owing to unequal distribution of educational and economic opportunities, a large portion of population suffered and thereby remained socially and educationally backward. Backwardness, developed either owing to economic causes or embodiment in socio-religious conditions, was a stumbling block in the way of national progress and unity. The Constitution, therefore, endeavours to eradicate backwardness by providing special facilities to backward sections of people. The Constitution has included detailed provisions to identify backward classes (SC & ST). The list of such classes is prepared and periodically looked into under Articles 335, 341, and 342. Care and precaution have been taken to identify and provide special facilities to the backward people. In order to ameliorate social conditions of the backward people, the Constitution gives priority to economic facilities and has enacted Article 16(4) and later the (Champakarn case) Article 15(4) was added. The main objective of Articles 15(4) and 16(4) is to foster equality by adopting a technique of adjusting socially and educationally weaker sections of the society and those who are socially and educationally strong. The only technique is to help them compete in areas pertaining to education and government employment. Reservation or compensatory discrimination or protective discrimination is justified in our social and economic conditions till the weaker sections of society are able to complete without any social help. The vital problem with which the States as well as courts are involved is the identification of the persons who are educationally and socially backward and are entitled to Constitutional benefit.

The problem has not yet been solved from *Balaji*[4] case till today as the criteria adopted by the states in most of the cases were found to be based on caste which is a prohibited criterion. In this case the Supreme Court invalidated the criteria as being based on caste. The Supreme Court in *Chitralekha* case upholding the decision of *Balaji* case observed that "if classes as specified in Article 15(4) were treated as castes the whole object of the Constitution would be frustrated."[5] But the Supreme Court in *Rajendran* case[6] gave liberal interpretation of caste. In *Sagar*[7] and *Periakaruppan*[8] cases, the court reiterated that a caste has always been treated as class and that the list of backward classes might validly be specified by caste only. It, therefore, indicates that the Supreme Court due to social complexities treated caste as class and class as caste.

Another issue of distinction between caste and class is of great legal and social significance. These two have different sociological effect and "class" has been included in Articles 15(4) and 16(4) because it has mobility whereas "caste" is a stagnant concept. There is no possibility of shifting a person of one caste to another caste. Caste system generates a feeling of separatism, a sense of superiority on religious ground whereas the concept of class has opposite effects and tendencies.

Caste criterion is not only constitutionally prohibited but also sociologically undesirable. The poverty criterion as indicated by the Jammu & Kashmir court was accepted by the Supreme Court in *Janki Prasad* case in India. Social backwardness was associated with economic backwardness,

4. *M.R.V. Balaji* vs. *State of Mysore, A.I.R.* 1963 SC. 49.
5. *V. Chitraleka* vs. *State of Mysore, A.I.R.* 1964 SC. 1823.
6. *P. Rajendran* vs. *State of Madras, A.I.R.* 1968, SC. 1012.
7. *State of Andhra Pradesh* vs. *Sagar, A.I.R.* 1968 SC. 1379.
8. *V. Periakaruppan* vs. *State of Tamil Nadu, A.I.R.* 1971 SC. 2303.

but the court refrained from adopting this criterion because it would make a very large proportion of population backward. But the court broke new ground in the matter of education saying that it is a cardinal element in social equipment. This criterion may pose problem when applied, as the adoption of education is the basis of classification would include a vast number of illiterates. Education as the basis to determine social backwardness could be a suitable criterion as the evil of casteism would be eliminated and suitable formula for the application of discrimination could be evolved.

Another issue attached to the problem of protective discrimination is the extent of reservation. Articles 15(4) and 16(4) permit reservation but are silent on this issue. It may be a deliberate omission because of the fluctuating conditions of the SCs and STs from one State to another. On this very issue *Balaji* case may be referred in which the Supreme Court considered Articles 15(4) and 16(4) as exceptions to articles 15(1) and 16(1) and held that the extent of reservation should not exceed 50 per cent of the total number of available posts. The Supreme Court in *Rangachari,*[9] *Balaji* and *Devdasan*[10] pointed out that general efficiency of administration or general interest should not be allowed to suffer at the cost of excessive reservations. But in *Thomas* case,[11] the Court not only regarded Article 16(4) as not an exception to Article 16(1), but Hon'ble Justice Krishna Iyer and Hon'ble Justice Murtaza Ali said that the extent of reservation might be as high as 80 per cent. *Thomas* case can be regarded as having gone too far as compared to

9. *General Manager* vs. *Rangachari, A.I.R.* SC. 36.

10. *Devadasan* vs. *Union of India* 1964 4 S.C.R. 680; *State of M.P.vs. Nivedita Jain, A.I.R.* 1981 SC. 298; *K.P. Ganguli* vs. *State of Kerala, A.I.R.* 1985 SC. 1495; *Aarti Gupta* vs. *State of Punjab, A.I.R.* 1988 SC. 481; *Fazal Ghafoor* vs. *Union of India, A.I.R.* 1989 SC. 481.

11. *State of Kerala* vs. *Thomas, A.I.R.* 1976 SC. 470.

Balaji case and **ignored** to maintain a balance between competing interests and the policy of protective discrimination. *Balaji* dealt with the problem in a more reasonable way. In *S. Chottey Lal*[12] case, the Supreme Court stayed the Allahabad High Court judgment which had struck down the Uttar Pradesh Government's order making reservation for persons belonging to backward classes in the state judicial services. The High Court upheld the reservation for the SCs and others while striking down part of the State Government's order that applied to backward classes and the court regarded Kurmis and Aheers and others mentioned in the government orders as not backward classes within the meaning of Article 16(4). This analysis indicates the manner in which the criteria of backwardness and the problem of adjustment of competing interests were dealt with by the judiciary.

The reservation issue popularly known as the Mandal imbroglio has caught everyone in a catch-22 situation when V.P. Singh, during his tenure as the Prime Minister, announced in Parliament on 9 August 1990, his decision of reserving certain percentage (27%) of all government jobs for "backward classes." The decision was then welcomed by all political parties. The decision was met with stray opposition in the beginning, but by the second half of September, the resentment exploded into an upper class movement with widespread violence and self-immolations in the northern belt. After two months, V.P. Singh's minority government fell. The nine member Constitution Bench of the Supreme Court of India delivered its historic judgement in the Reservation Case related to Socially and Educationally Backward Classes (SEBCs) popularly known as "Mandal Case" on 16 November 1992. The case arose out of several writ petitions challenging the

12. *Chottey Lal* vs. *State of U.P., A.I.R.* 1979 1-11, 135.

Office Memoranda of August 13, 1990 and 25 September 1991 issued by the Government of India for implementing the recommendations of reservation for SEBC's in public employment. The recommendations were made by the Second Backward Classes Commission appointed under Article 340 of the Constitution popularly known as the Mandal Commission. The Court held that the Office Memorandum of 13 August 1990 providing for reservation in civil services and posts under the Government of India in favour of other backward classes would be valid and enforceable subject to the exclusion of the "creamy layer" from the notified "Other Backward Classes." The Government constituted an Expert Committee under the Chairmanship of Justice Ram Nandan Prasad, a retired judge from Patna High Court on 22 February 1993, to specify the criteria for the identification of socially advanced persons among the SEBCs. The expert committee submitted its report to the government on 10 March 1993. The then Welfare Minister Shri Sitaram Kesri made a statement in Parliament on 16 March announcing the government's decision to accept the recommendations contained in the report. The report unequivocally held that the denial of reservation to any member of SEBCs was to be treated only as an exception; it had to be ensured that the ill-effects had been fully and finally eliminated and that no grey area was discernible. The Committee said that it would be proper and desirable to allow some acceleration and coverage of the same distance in reservation before the brake is applied. The Expert Committee concluded that, only when the creamy layer is substantially stable and crosses the threshold of social backward stigma; then and then alone can it be made the basis for disentitlement.[13]

---

13. *Rashtriya Sahara*, November 1994.

The recommendations were as follows:

(a) The Committee said that the rule of exclusion will apply to the posts of President, Vice-President, Judges of the Supreme Court and High Courts, Chairman/ Members of UPSC and SPSC, Chief Election Commissioner, Comptroller and Auditor General and other posts of similar nature.

(b) For the service category the committee said if either of the spouses is a Class I officer, the rule of exclusion will apply. Where both spouses are Class I officers and one of them dies, the situation remains unchanged and the rule of exclusion will apply. However, if both of them die, the children shall not be denied the benefit of reservation and the rule of exclusion will not apply to them. Referring to Group B Class II Central and States Service, the committee said that if both spouses are Class II officers, it will not apply, but if a male officer from the Class II category gets into Class I Category at the age of 40 or earlier, it will apply to his offspring. Where both spouses are Class II officers and one of them dies the rule of exclusion will not apply. However, if either of the spouses had the benefit of employment in any international organization for a period of not less than 5 years then even in the events of death, the application of the role of exclusion will not apply to the offspring.

Where the husband is a Class I officer and the wife is a Class II officer and the husband dies, the rule of exclusion will apply. The rule of exclusion will apply on the principle that of the parents namely, the mother continues to be a Class I officer,

The nine judges bench issued six separate judgments (in 911 pages). These should be treated as an erudite exposition of judicial creativity in tune with constitutional objectivity. The judges argued that as economic backwardness was the bane of the majority of the people in this country, poverty by itself cannot be the test of backwardness as most of the people would then be in a position to claim reservation, and reservation for all was reservation for more. Reservation was meant to remedy the historical injustice and the persisting evil effects of historical discrimination. Mere economic and educational backwardness which was not the result of social backwardness could not be the criteria of "backwardness" under Article 16(4) and economic criteria might be a consideration along with and in addition to social backwardness.

(c) With regard to backwardness, the objective is to locate and identify social backwardness and the effort should be to consider all the available groups, sections and classes of society in whichever order our effort may proceed. This can be followed by applying the criteria backwardness evolved and having exhausted the costs or simultaneously, taking up for consideration other occupational groups, communities and classes. As the backward classes for purposes of Article 16(4) must not only be socially backward, but also inadequately represented in the services under the state, implied in any procedure for their identification is the imperative to ascertain this inadequacy as well. In a backward class under Article 16(4), if some members are far too advanced socially, the connecting thread between them and the remaining class snaps. There would be misfits in the class. The exclusion should not be on economic basis, but on the basis of social advancement, unless of course, the economic advancement is so high that it necessarily meant the latter. Keeping in view various considerations, they directed the Central Government to specify the basis for the exclusion of the "creamy layer" as early as possible.

On the sub-classification of the OBCs, there were three different views.The primary one was social backwardness; such classification was not permissible and valid. As long as there was a substantial difference in the backwardness of the backward classes, it was imperative to make the sub-classification if the latter were to gain equitable benefits of reservation. The basis for classification should be the degree of social backwardness and not an economic consideration and that if backward classes were so classified, the separate quotas of reservation would have to be kept for such classes. As the identification of the backward classes was to offer them the benefit of reservations what should follow logically is a close look at the nature and the extent of reservation for them. That reservation should be a one time offer confined only to initial appointments would be a serious and unacceptable inroad into the rule of equality of opportunity. Reservation in promotion would operate only prospectively and not affect promotions already made. Reservations wherever already provided in promotions in the central, state and related services would continue in operation for 5 years from the date of ruling and within this period it would be open to the authorities to revise or re-issue the relevant rules to ensure the achievement of the objective of Article 16(4).

(d) As regards the extent of overall reservation, it must remain below 50 per cent and under no circumstances should it exceed this limit. The validity of the percentage to reservation would depend upon the size of backward classes as long as it was not so excessive as to virtually obliterate the claims of others under Article 16(1). It was not open to challenge and there was no legal infirmity in keeping the reservations under Articles 16(4) and 16(1) together exceeding 50 per cent. Relating to 50 per cent rule for the purpose of application, one year should be the unit and not the entire strength of the cadre, service or the wait as the case may be and the carry forward, in whatever manner it was operated, should not result in the breach of this rule. Any objection to the criteria that might be evolved for excluding the creamy layer . . . and for classification of the OBCs into backward and more backward classes for equitable distribution of the benefits, and any petition questioning the validity of the two impugned orders on any grounds should be instituted only before the apex court.

There were certain limitations. The OBCs eligible for reservation were those not adequately represented in the services under the State; the matter of adequacy was a matter within the subjective satisfaction of the appropriate government, and the judiciary had not laid down any method for ascertaining this aspect. The decision of the judiciary was that reservation could be made by an executive order and need not necessarily be the decision of parliament or Legislature. Though the executive order may be valid, since a Constitutional provision was being implemented for the first time after 1950–1990, propriety demanded that it should have been placed before the parliament to lay down healthy convention. In a number of states no effort at identification of the OBCs had been made; so the question of the State Lists and the Mandal List "marrying" could not arise, and as such there would be a breakdown of implementation.

Outweighing these very limitations were four important aspects of these rulings. First, the rule of 50 per cent ceiling, earlier regarded as *obiter dicta*, put a break on the direction that the courts were taking in expanding the extent of reservations, and reversed that trend so as to strike a proper balance; secondly, exclusion of the "creamy layer" gradually rationalized and depractised the reservation policy, discouraged the growth of vested interest in reservations and helped in accelerating the advancement of the "really backward." Thirdly, the overall ceiling of reservation at 50 per cent confined only to the "really backward" and to initial appointment would gradually convince the anti-reservationists that there was no scope for abusing the reservation policy and would help in overcoming their aggressive anti-reservation postures. Fourthly, in States and Union Territories where reservations did not exist, the OBCs were expected to get the benefit of reservations under the new dispensation.

Despite these anticipated positive effects, the implementation of the ruling is likely to be very difficult because of four reasons. Firstly, politicians in States where reservations are in excess of 50 per cent (69 to 79) are bound to build pressure against the ceiling and the exclusion of the "creamy layer" and for continuing reservations in promotions. Secondly, while inclusion in the lists of the OBCs by the committee to be appointed would be smooth, exclusion of any group from the existing lists would be resisted. Thirdly, considering that the Central Government had failed to present to the court its much talked about economic criteria, owing to which hearing was adjourned more than once, it is doubtful that it would do so in the near future. Since the reservations can not be implemented unless these criteria are evolved and approved by the judiciary, the delay may in effect shelve the judgements as well. Fourthly, the move of the Central Government to seek a Constitutional amendment for circumventing the court order down the 10 per cent reservation for the economically backward was recommended even by the so-called "Champion of the Backward Classes."

There is a world of difference between judicial pragmatism and political opportunism. Politicians, as a class, are concerned more with power than with the backward sections of the society. It is the moot point whether the judiciary has finally and authoritatively settled the reservation issue. But as long as judicial arguments and decrees are not translated into reality, the OBCs will never be delivered from their historic plight.

The Supreme Court has tried to provide a new approach to the problem of reservation especially the recent decision, viz. *Ajit Singh* vs. *State of Punjab* and others.

The Supreme Court has tried to bring a balancing act amidst competing and conflicting interests amongst employees belonging to the open category on one hand and reserved category on the other. The Supreme Court, in its decision, pointed out that:

> It is so heartening to note that for whom the founding fathers introduced the provision for reservation to protect and encourage entry in service, now are able to enter service on their own merit by competing with candidates of general category. For promotion or appointment of a member of Scheduled Caste against the post reserved for him, the primary question to be considered is as to whether he belongs to a class for whom reservation has been made. But for being considered for appointment or promotion against

> a general category post, merit is the primary consideration because the applicant is to enter into the service or trade of service through merit channel.[14]

Further the decision has highlighted that,

> When framers of the Constitution by Article 16 guaranteed equality of opportunity in matters of public employment, they aimed at combining democratization with efficiency. In the process of democratization, Article 16(4) of the Constitution enabled the State to make provisions for reservation of appointments or posts in favour of any backward class of citizens, which in the opinion of the State, is not adequately represented in the services under the State.[15]

Broadly speaking the legal point behind its decision was that:

> All concerned who are involved and interested in the uplift and growth of the nation have to work out a system by which the injustice done to a section of people in our society at certain period of history can be rectified by providing protections to their descendants. But we have to be conscious at the same time that the efficiency of the administration of the country is not harmed and there is no reverse discrimination.[16]

This was in tune with the principles of social democracy championed by Ambedkar. The decision further explained the principle of equality in the new context and had noted that:

> The equality principle requires exclusion of the factor of extra-weightage of earlier promotion to a reserved category candidate because of reservation alone, when he competes

14. *Ajit Singh Januja and others* vs. *State of Panjab, A.I.R.* 1996 SC. 1199.
15. Ibid., p. 1200 (para 15).
16. Ibid.

> for further promotion to a general category with a general category candidate senior to him in the panel. Any other view would amount to reverse discrimination and violative of the guarantee of equality under Articles 14 to 16.[17]

Thus Ambedkar's vision and philosophy of social justice has been reinterpreted by Hon'ble Supreme Court in a relevant manner.

In conclusion, the recommendations of the Mandal Commission may be beneficial but within the limits laid down by the judiciary. But in view of the multi-dimensional problems faced particularly by the middle classes such as shrinking of jobs, marked growth of population and increase in quota, the question of reservation needs a fresh look and another commission having representation from all States at the earliest. The task to study the problem of identifying the OBCs with extreme care and caution must not be ignored.

---

17. Ibid.

5

His Fight for Rights and Values

THERE is a lot to be learnt from Ambedkar's political life. He made a unique and significant contribution to the fight of the untouchables. Hitherto, the untouchables relied on social reformers and caste Hindus to hold their brief for them. Ambedkar ensured that the untouchables became a viable political fighting force that was to be reckoned with. It was not an easy task. He was pitted against one of the greatest and cleverest politicians of the twentieth century. He both won and lost. He lost the skirmish, won the battle and lost the war. The Poona Pact was the skirmish. The fact that he got joint electorates meant that he won the battle. But, over a period of time, he was not totally able to prevent the untouchables from being absorbed into the Congress. That was the war. He lost it. Clearly any initiative would have to go far beyond. A new war has to be launched to fight for the rights of the untouchables. This new war must use tactics which go far beyond a simple demand for electoral representation in designated institutions. There is no doubt, however, that the philosophy underlying Ambedkar's strategy is still very important; soon after the Poona Pact, when Ambedkar discovered the express and implied limitations of his own political initiative, he fought on. He constantly reminded Gandhi about the needs of the untouchables and expressed their political and social separateness brilliantly with his dramatic threat of conversion at Yeola. His constant attempts to establish breakway political parties also demonstrate his desire to keep the untouchability movement a distinct political force in Indian society. But while he was an effective campaigner and was politically adept at handling many of the events which he managed with skill, he was not able to create the administrative and political machinery to consolidate and strengthen the work of the political parties which he had created.

Ambedkar was not just another minority leader. He was a minority leader with a message. In order to evaluate his message, it is necessary to return to his distinction between fighting for rights and fighting for values.

In terms of practical politics the significance of the distinction is that the minority in question is asked to retain an independent political viability. This might tend to suggest that Ambedkar was also arguing that a minority should never wholly join mainstream politics. Ambedkar was not laying down a once-and-for-all pattern for all or any political campaigns which a minority group might want to pursue. In the context of India and of the fight of the untouchables he thought that there were too many dangers in the untouchables joining the Congress and relying on the internal politics of the Congress to obtain what they wanted. In different circumstances and for the campaign of a different kind of minority, it could, perhaps be perfectly proper to use mainstream political parties to achieve the ends of that particular minority. In each case, however, Ambedkar suggests that the minority in question should watch out for certain dangers. This biggest danger is the very strong possibility that the people, groups and institutions of mainstream politics would try and take over the political initiative of the minority. This, in Ambedkar's view, would diminish and eventually destroy the political viability of the minority.

Most minorities are faced with a dual fight on their hands. The first fight is simply to gain certain privileges and to get help to overcome certain disadvantages. The second fight is against the majority itself and consists of an attempt to persuade (or force) the majority to stop being discriminatory. The first fight is a relatively easy one since it just consists of asking for various kinds of compensatory advantages by arguing that such advantages can only be given to a limited extent. This is argued partly on the basis that an extensive lay-out of compensatory advantages and privileges would militate against notions of equality. Consequently, the bigger the claims for compensatory advantages and privileges, the greater the need for a strong justification, and unequivocal proof that such compensatory advantages and privileges are necessary. Undoubtedly, the capacity of minority to political pressure would greatly influence the majority to yield to an extensive demand for compensatory discrimination and privileges. The second kind of fight does not simply consist of asking the majority for certain kinds of favours. It is a fight against the majority itself. It accuses the majority of being discriminatory. The purpose of this second fight is to try and ensure that the majority change their behaviour and attitude towards the minority.

Ambedkar felt that the first kind of fight was simply picking up crumbs from the majority's table. It was the second kind of fight, that was the real fight. It consisted of persuading, embarrassing, pressurizing and where possible forcing the majority to change their attitude. Ambedkar deplored that if the you-can't-beat-'em join'em attitude of minorities. He was the majority by favours, concessions and even in limited cases, agreeing to some changes in the majority's attitude to the minority. Ambedkar wanted the second kind of fight would have to be disguised so as to seem as if it was not a fight. But the fight was a fight, and it was wrong to treat the minority in any other way.

Since Ambedkar's approach was not just concerned with matters of political strategy, it is also important to consider the deeper implications of the distinction between the fight for rights and the fight for values. One way to approach the problem is to demonstrate that there is a positive and complementary relationship between these two kinds of fights. Let us take an example. When members of a black community in a society fight with a white majority against racism along with some white members of that society, they are both fighting for their rights as well as for certain egalitarian values. It might be to the advantage of this black minority to combine their fights with the fight of those white folk who are opposed to racism and who are therefore, fighting for the attainment of the same egalitarian values. It could be further argued that since both the groups of people are fighting for the same thing, the real fight is the fight for values and the fight for rights is no more than a part of the general fight for the preservation of these values. All this seems to suggest that rights and values can never be in conflict. This is a very dangerous suggestion which we need to examine.

A right is claim to do, or refrain from doing something. This claim may be made by a person or group. Now, for a large variety of reasons not all claims can be permitted. But let us consider the basis on which rights and their exercise are limited. The first basis for the limitation of rights is simply the *de facto* existence of power. People who have power over others can, under certain circumstances, simply use their power to impose restrictions on those who are powerless to fight back. In such cases, the restrictions are on those who are powerless to fight back. In such cases, the restrictions imposed on rights take place solely on the basis that one person or group chooses to exercise their power over another person or group without justifying this on any basis other than pointing out the differential in their relative power. More often than not, the limitation of rights does not formally taken place on "I have power and-you-do-not" basis. This takes us to the second basis on which limitations are imposed on rights. Apart from power, limitations on rights are justified on the basis of values. Thus, rights can be limited on the basis of the value attached to the rights of others. Again, rights may be limited on the basis of the value attached to some policy or to some aspect of the legal order. The sum total of these restrictions may, in the long run, even assist the exercise of some rights. But it's values which are used to determine which rights (or claims) are to be accepted by society and what kind of restriction society can and should impose on such rights (or claims). Indeed, apart from power, there is no other social basis on which limitations can be imposed on rights and their exercise. Values are, therefore, antithetical to rights in that, apart from power, values form the only basis on which the limitation of rights can be justified.

Values represent the framework within which demand for rights are negotiated. Sometimes there may be good reason for the imposition of certain limitations, sometimes there may not be. Values play a very crucial role in the social validation of rights. No doubt, the premium put on certain values is influenced by the power *status quo* in any society. It is difficult to assert that power exercises more influence over the human mind and human society than an appeal to values. Both play an important role in the social validation of rights.

People fighting for their rights are taught to fear power. They are told that the only real threat to their rights is power. In actual fact, a naked unequivocal exercise of power, though a danger in itself, is not the biggest normal day-to-day threat to rights. Since rights cannot always be absolute, every society seeks to limit rights on the basis of values.

Ambedkar visualized the Congress and Hindu society drawing up all kinds of values on the basis of which rights of the untouchable could be limited. The utilitarian needs of the day, the demands of policy imperatives, the cultural traditions of India, the need for law and order, the scarcity of resources and appeal to rationality were all set up as good reasons for the limitation of the rights of the untouchable. Ambedkar seemed to warn the untouchables that they would be deprived of their rights not just through the exercises of power but also by insidious appeals to values. Hindu society with its emphasis on duties and its respect for particular kind of social order represented an uncompromising network of values. Ambedkar rightly thought that it was best to fight this entire network of values rather than to campaign for piecemeal and minor changes.

Values determine the basis on which the rights of people are limited. But, values are the product of human thought and social compromise. Those fighting for their rights must be very wary of the values which are used to limit their rights. These values, and the social circumstances which give rise to them, must be constantly scrutinized and, where necessary, vigorously opposed.

AMBEDKAR'S VIEWS ON ARTICLE 356 OF THE CONSTITUTION

Ambedkar scaled heights in his life (1891–1956) which baffled common imagination. He sprang from background, born into an untouchable caste, shudras of Hindu society. Realities some time suppress dreams in their enchantment.

Ordinarily, a man born among the untouchable, shudras, is doomed forever. The code of Manu, governing lives of the

Hindus, legitimized all sorts of insults and cruelties against him. His touch, even his shadow, will defile the person of a high caste Hindu, who will be obliged to take bath immediately. The shudra will keep off the roads used by superior Hindus. Nor will he drink water from community wells and tanks of the village or town. In order to quench his thirst, he will go to the pond where cattle and dogs usually drank water. Manu took special care to deny education to the untouchables and prescribed most severe punishment if they tried to gain familiarity with the holy scriptures, the Vedas. Further, Manu commanded the high caste Hindus not to treat the untouchable with sympathy. They had been destined for humbler duties: sweeping, scavenging, and carrying dirty refuse over their heads. There could be no amelioration of the miseries of these sons and daughters of Mother India.

Ambedkar grew up in an environment of utter despondency. His biographer has assiduously put together all relevant details of Ambedker's career. In boyhood, he displayed indomitable will-power to face physical hardship accompanying social disabilities, and thus, successfully crossed the stage of primary education (up to 1915). Success in higher studies, pursued in United States of America, Germany, and England, revealed itself owing to a combination of factors, chiefly, his own hard work. Having returned to India with brilliant academic record, a doctorate in economics and the usual barrister's degree, he made teaching his first choice. As the hate campaign of high caste Hindus made it impossible for him to stick to teaching he turned to the Bar. After the end of the First World War, political activities gathered momentum. To every young man of legal discipline, politics offered a good opening and Ambedkar did not lose the opportunity.

Naturally, his focus of attention was the plight of his own people, the untouchables. The arena summoning him was not the popular freedom movement against British domination, but freedom of the oppressed classes from social bondage. Oppression of the high caste Hindus was the main challenge. His status was secured as the Governor of Bombay nominated him a member of the Legislative Council (1926).

The first opportunity of his life arose when he led ten thousand untouchables to drink water from a public tank at the town of Mahad, Maharashtra. In its audacity the step of the leader was remarkable, and the action brought immense courage to his people. The orthodox purified the tank by pouring a mixture of cow dung and cow urine into its water (1927). Significantly, at that stage he thought of advising his followers to embrace some other religion. He told the high caste Hindus: "If you say, your religion is our religion, then, your rights and our rights must be equal."[1] Furthermore, "what was the worth of the religion which treated its own adherents as worse than dogs."[2]

As a strategist and man of action, he knew the difficulty of opening two fronts. He, therefore, kept peace with the British. He appeared to give evidence before the Southborough Commission appointed by Montague, Secretary of State of India and proposed separate electorate for the untouchables.[3]

As the Simon Commission arrived, and it made two visits in 1928 and 1929, the Congress boycotted it. Nonetheless, Ambedkar extended his co-operation. In his evidence he supported "Joint electorates with reservation of seats for the

---

1. Dhananjay Keer, *Ambedkar : His Life and Mission*, 2nd edn., 1992.
2. Ibid., p. 92.
3. Ibid., p. 40.

depressed classes."[4] This departure from his earlier stand was a step towards conciliation with upper-caste Hindus (1928).

The belligerent mood revived again at the time of the Round Table Conferences: 1930 and 1931. From the first, the Congress was deliberately absent. In the second, while Gandhiji appeared claiming his party and himself to be the sole representative of India and the Indians — i.e. including the untouchables, the Muslims and all others — his most vocal opponent was Ambedkar. The latter's relentless attacks did not fail to invite notice of the British Press and parliamentarians. He pleaded for "separate electorate to the untouchables," for it was a unanimous demand of all their associations in various parts of the country.

No consensus emerged at the conferences. But, at the close of the second conference, the British Prime Minister, Ramsay Macdonald, obtained signatures from leaders of all communities, including Gandhi, whereby they committed themselves to the decision of the British Government. Seven months thereafter was announced the famous Communal Award. It granted separate electorates to all minorities and also to the untouchables.

The political crisis resulting from the Award was inevitable. Gandhi resorted to fast unto death on the plea that it would create "perpetual division in Hindu society." All Hindu leaders, congressmen, conservatives and liberals joined hands to exert influence on Ambedkar. He was in a dilemma. On the one hand were the benefits of separate electorates, and on the other was the life of India's great leader bent on self-annihilation. At last Ambedkar yielded to the common wishes. Gandhi's life was saved and the offer of communal award was given up. Instead of "separate electorate," it was agreed

4. Ibid., p. 115.

to give more reservation to the untouchables. The agreement with the Congress came to be called "Poona Pact." From that time onward Ambedkar found all offices of prestige and power accessible to him. Nonetheless, as remarked by his biographer, the "Poona Pact" closed an epoch.[5]

A man's self-development may carry him through many zigzag paths, which apparently resemble opportunism. Only knowledge of the situation could offer the correct answer. Particularly, if he emerged as a man of action, the opposing sentiments of pious dedication and personal ambition will force him at every step to resolve these contradictions with rare exceptions. Such a human type could afford to be an iconoclast and a transparent revolutionary. In his scheme, pleading was better than fighting and compromise, a possibility replacing confrontation. Ambedkar's life confirmed the soundness of these points; and the story of his career revealed that adaptability rather than outright aggressiveness was his guiding principle.

Briefly, his chief mission was one. To deliver the untouchables from sub-human conditions and raise them to social equality. For the attainment of this single object, the open courses were two. First, staying in the Hindu-fold and seeking redress at both legal and social planes, invoke government machinery and also launch social reform movement against discrimination. Secondly, if the above-mentioned efforts belied hope, abandon Hinduism and embrace another religion.

As regards the first course, with legal remedy contained therein, its climax was reached at the time of Communal Award (1932) when the British Government granted separate electorate to the untouchables, later on called Harijans.

5. Ibid., p. 216.

Ambedkar surrendered the benefits back. After some time, realizing his error of judgement he secretly voyaged to England and raised the issue again. Nobody was interested in listening to the old argument that the untouchables were a separate element. The British politicians "advised him to adjust himself" with the upper caste Hindus.[6]

The other remedy, linked to the first option, was the social reform movement. It continued from a number of platforms in a prudent fashion. Nor was the top leadership of the Congress impervious to it. Nonetheless side by side with the weight of the reformers and the might of independent India's Constitution, Manu's law defiantly stood intact.

To try the second course was not without logic, and the ideal had firm grasp over Ambedkar's mind. But, like all other shrewd politicians, he exercised the approved method of one step forward, two steps backward. Wrangling with high caste Hindus and bitter complaints against them went on parallel with publicity for change of religion. The drama attracted the attention of Christians, Muslims, Sikhs, and finally, the Buddhists. A few months before his death, Ambedkar embraced Buddhism (1956) saying; "It was the least harmful way for the country." Nor were the high caste Hindus perturbed by his action. For, as pronounced by Radhakrishnan, "Buddhism was purer Hinduism."[7] Outside India, his book on the subject, *Buddha and His Gospel*, instead of winning praise, was bluntly condemned by Buddhist authorities. Inside the country, the caste Hindus gradually got accustomed to his cries of protest on the question of social inequality and derisively called them: "noise of a mill."[8]

---

6. Ibid., p. 383.
7. Dhananjay Keer, *Ambedkar and His Mission*, p. 428.
8. Ibid.

Tragically, the drawbacks found in the making of the Constitution originated from the author's deep-rooted habit and life-long training. In his calculation, flexibility was a valuablemerit and to please the Congress bosses a necessity. They, in return, reciprocated him with gifts and honours. The last and most memorable gift was the Chairmanship of the Drafting Committee of India's Constitution.

Of all the parts bearing the frame of the Constitution, Part 18, "Emergency Provisions," seems to have caused more than usual apprehension in the minds of its architects. The said part carries nine articles. Among them, Article 356 has made itself conspicuous owing to its profuse size; it is the lengthiest single article. Actually, the load of words invested in its construction has made it structurally precarious.

Frugality in the use of words is the first precautionary demand of common sense. For, equate often they tend to upon clarity. Mind once unsure and baffled has no recourse save. The members of Drafting Committee faced similar situation when they settled down to design Part 18 of the Constitution, particularly Article 356 integrated therein. It was evident from the objections raised by some of them[9] and the discussion that followed that they had a feeling of uneasiness in regard to the said article and were critical of the inherent flaw in it. They were aware that every word must be open to judicial interpretation which in turn would open Pandora's box. However, they did not insist on downright rejection, modification, or softening of the article. Discreetly it was left to future generations to relish or disdain the taste of Article 356.

Notwithstanding the abundant vision which Ambedkar was supposed to possess, he seemed to have shown himself

9. H.V. Kamath, *Constitution Assembly Debates*, vol. 9, p. 140.

the least organization in the framing of Article 356. In a generalized way the same thing may be said about the Constitution as a whole. However, let us concede that following the narrow path of the Government of India Act, 1935 was not his free option. It was a demoracted and dictated policy. But, the articles of Part 18 during the moment of enactment posed real challenge to the learned professor's genius. Oddly enough, he simply picked up Article 278 of the Government of India Act, 1935 and placed it in the existing Constitution as Article 356. No botheration was deemed necessary to convince himself and others that the makers of the above mentioned Article 278 (the British Members of the House of Commons and former rulers of India) had vanished from scene, their motives and intentions in making the said article must be altogether different, the times and conditions had changed and the second world war intervened as an awful between 1935 and the years after 1947. And, above all, the constitution of free India was being drafted for its people living in one vast land where the difference between British India and Princely India were no more. Moreover, the remarks of Ambedkar during the debates betrayed that he was hafl-hearted in the matter of full and strong protection allowed to the units (States) from encroachment by the centre. Once he remarked:[10]

> I think it is agreed that our Constitution, notwithstanding the many provision which are contained in it, whereby the centre has been given powers to override the provinces, none-theless, is a federal Constitution and when we say that the provinces (States) are sovereign[11] in their field which is left to them by the Constitution as the centre is in the field which

10. Ibid., p. 133.
11. The Supreme Court rejected the idea in its verdict: *State of West Bengal* vs. *Union of India, A.I.R.* 1963 SC. 1214.

> is assigned to it. In other words, barring the provisions which permit the centre to override any legislation that may be passed by the provinces (States) have a plenary powers to make any law for the peace, order and good government of that province (State), really speaking, the intervention of the centre or any other authority must be deemed to be barred, because that would be an invasion of the sovereign authority of that province (State). That is a fundamental proposition which I think, we must accept by reason of the fact that we have a federal Constitution. That being so, if the centre is to interfere in the administration of the provincial (State) affairs, as we propose to authorize the centre by virtue of Article 278 (356) and Article 277A (357), it must be by and under some obligation, which the Constitution imposes upon the centre. The invasion must not be an invasion which is wanton, arbitrary and unauthorized by law.

Hereunder is another example of the professor's enfeebled will so far as emergency provisions were concerned. He said:

> In regard to the general debate which had taken place in which it has been suggested that those articles are likely to be abused, I may say that I do not deny altogether that there is possibility of these articles being abused or employed for political purpose. But that objection applies to every part of the Constitution which gives power to the centre to override the provinces (States).[12]

Serving as solid foundation for the edifice, Article 355 was introduced prior to the article we are discussing. Its introduction preceding Article 356, left no doubt as to the overriding authority of the centre in relation to states. In fact, it had already found its due place as Article 277A in the Government of India Act, 1935. Picking up from there was again an act amounting to casually or original thinking. As

---

12. *Constituent Assembly* Debates, vol. 9, p. 177.

regards the British rulers, they were justified in the enactment of Article 277A, for, it was their deliberate calculation to keep the "provinces," where power was supposed to pass to democratically elected Indians, under permanent stress. Needless to say "the provinces" were made more vulnerable to centre's invasion. But, when the Constitution of free India was drafted, conditions had changed. Time has proved that the warning signals by some of the members of the constituent assembly deserved to be paid more careful attention. Nobody would hesitate to answer the question now, whether perpetuating the old situation caused more harm than good. Lack of consideration for others' rights was the one peculiar habit of the colonial master. And, as regards "emergency provisions" of our Constitution, the Indian rulers at the centre have repeatedly and unhesitatingly exhibited that something close to the awkward colonial habit has still survived intact.

It has been an accepted principle amply justified by experience that in big countries of subcontinental dimensions federalism provides more convenient and workable feature to the governments. In case of India, the makers of our Constitution were fully conscious of this fact. From the beginning, they professed that they will not permit the Constitutional frame to lose its federal shape. Balancing between the centre and the States was almost like walking on the tight rope indeed. By and large, the members of the Drafting Committee adhered to their declared object. Leaving aside minor provisions where their bias in favour of the centre came to the surface, it was the framing of part 18, precisely Article 356 of the above-mentioned part, where their steps became unsteady. They seemed to be losing sight of their definite path. Alone this article must be deemed responsible to have changed the complexion and influenced the spirit of the entire Constitution. Its insertion, together with the preceding and suceeding ones, has put a serious question mark against federalism. Many intelligent man, not convinced by what the Constitution claimed, floated other and more intelligible phrases, for example, "*quasi-federal.*" A modern Constitutional expert has made the most appropriate and bold comment. He observed, "of the various provisions of the Constitution which have resulted in diluting the principle of federalism in India, Article 356 has yielded the worst consequences."[13]

Let us recall that an exceptional situation was created by Article 356 when it exposed the whole Constitution to general amusement and laughter. Keeping in view that nothing demands greater restraint and caution from the Parliament than the attempt to amend the Constitution, two such attempts, ultimately proving futile and fruitless, were made in connection with the above-mentioned article. One, the Constitution 35th Amendment Bill 1975, expressly prohibited the judicial authority of the country from taking cognizance of Presidential Proclamations issued under Article 356. Such a proclamation was declared as "beyond the scope of judicial review in any court on any ground." Two, the Constitution's 44th Amendment Bill 1978 removed the impediment placed by the former 35th Amendment. The intelligentsia of the country witnessed both scenes with gapes. Indeed, the seriousness of the discipline of jurisprudence could hardly compromise itself with these opposing and fantastic exercises.

According to careful reckoning, from the commencement of the Constitution, 1950 to the year 1991, Presidential Proclamations under Article 356, causing to dismiss or suspend the State Government had been made 95 times.[14] A very

13. Tarkunde's Viewpoint, see *Hindustan Times*, 3 May 1994.

14. Ibid.

interesting and useful study by the Indian Law Institute, New Delhi appeared on this subject under the title: President's Rule in the States. Taking 86 cases of Presidential Proclamations, the study brought out how roughly Article 356 was used from the Nehru era down to the Janata Party rule. And now (1994) the number must have touched around one hundred. On the last occasion, during Narasimha Rao's regime, after demolition of Babri Masjid and the events that followed, the Madhya Pradesh High Court declared the Presidential Proclamation dismissing BJP ruled (Patwa) Government of the State as invalid by 2:1 majority. Subsequently, when the case covering the overall dismissal of six States, came for hearing before the Supreme Court, the Full Bench of nine Judges delivered five separate judgements. Clearly, such a situation may be called baffling from the standpoint of intelligent men only marginally interested in legal questions. It reminded everybody of the legend of the elephant and blind men.

Ironically, Ambedkar gave repeated assurances to the dissenting members of the Constituent Assembly that Article 356 would be very sparingly used. When the members pointed out that the article had great potential for inflicting harm, he frankly and disarmingly agreed with their fears. In reply, he tried to enlighten them with a lecture full of learning and wisdom:

> I share the sentiments expressed by my honourable friend Mr. Gupta yesterday that the proper thing we ought to expect is that such articles will never be called into operation and they would remain a dead letter. If at all they are brought into operation, I hope precautions would be taken before actually suspending the administration of the provinces. I hope the first thing he will do would be to issue warning to a province that has erred, that things were not happening in the way in which they were intended to happen in the

> Constitution. If that warning fails, the second thing for him to do will be to order an election allowing the people of the province to settle matters by themselves. It is only when these two remedies fail that he would resort to this article.[15]

In the context of the above exhortation Ambedkar left on record, a few critical observations should not be out of place. It will be idle to doubt his understanding of human nature, and similarly, his knowledge of the character possessed by men of action. Impatient, ambitious, dauntless, unscrupulous and ruthless to the core as had been men of power in the past, so shall they remain in the future. The conclusion, therefore, is not far to draw. A gifted thinker and scholar of political science, Ambedkar must be fully aware that the suggestions he made were merely theoretical. In the heat of practical expediency every Machiavelli incarnate will discard them and nobody will take their serious notice. So, why did he incorporate in letter and spirit Article 356 in the Constitution of free India would ever remain a paradox of legal history. Perhaps, ambivalence was his determined policy. Obviously, he could not earn much credit from serious scholars when they examined the nature of the said Article.[16]

Once, Katju, the Home Minister angrily snubbed Dr. Ambedkar: "you made the Constitution." And Ambedkar's reply was a rare specimen of frankness: "I was a hack, what I was to do, I did much against my will."[17]

---

15. *Constituent Assembly Debates*, supra, note 12.
16. H.M. Seervai, *Constitutional Law of India*, vol. 2, pp. 2624-29.
17. Supra, note 7, p. 447.

6

Ambedkar and Weaker Sections of Society

Baba Saheb, as we know, was an enemy of the caste system and Brahmanism. But often in his bleak moments he would advocate an escape from the caste-ridden Hindu system by advocating a change of religion if one's religion does not give status, dignity, equal treatment and a life of honour and grace. Adoption of a new religion becomes inevitable, which is fair and reasonable and ensures a place of honour and dignified living. Where a religion discriminates and confers no status, naturally a man would like to seek conversion to another religion which would save him from atrocities and exploitation and guarantee him a life like all others. Baba Saheb became a Buddhist by embracing Buddhism which is opposed to caste system. On 14 October 1994, it was reported that a number of Hindus including a few I.A.S. and I.P.S. officers would embrace Buddhism in the month of October 1994. Whether this action still solves the problem of the down-trodden people is yet to be known. It is said that mere change of religion by itself is no guarantee for conferring on them social status. This becomes possible only when political power comes in their hands. In the State of Uttar Pradesh, the sharing of power and struggle for power continue with political motives making the situation more pitiable sometimes. For Baba Saheb the priority was not how to integrate the social reform sub-agenda with the freedom struggle the overwhelming goal to which all other objectives must be subordinated. It was how to give centrality to the reform agenda as part of building a new equal, free, open and non-hierarchical modern India. He had no interest in making Hinduism or Hindu society shine forth.

Ambedkar was forthright when he stated: "we do not wish to live as shudras in the fourfold *varna* structure." He counterpoised caste in Hinduism to human dignity itself. In 1927, he burnt *Manusmriti*; in 1935, he denounced Shastras and declared an all-out war on caste which ultimately had led to the issue of reservations and caste war. Miss Mayawati and Sri Kanshiram have of late launched their tirades against brahmins, kshatriyas and vaishyas on the plea that owing to their Manuvadi tendencies, the Dalits could not get respectable position in society which they rightly deserved for a long time. How long would you expect them to wait to get those rights which the privileged class has been enjoying since time immemorial? Baba Saheb in *Annihilation of Caste* published in 1936 has narrated how atrocities were committed on the untouchables on flimsy grounds.

According to the *The Times of India* report of 17 May 1994 an average of ten cases of atrocities on Dalits were registered per day over the last three years in just the state of Rajasthan. Instances were not found lacking in other States also.

Ambedkar was determined to bring the backward classes in the mainstream of the nation, and their uplift in all spheres of life was his main concern. That is why being the chief architect of the Indian Constitution, he was particular about framing Article 16 which runs as follows:

1. There shall be equality of opportunity for all citizens (including untouchables, dalits, persons belonging to weaker sections — men and women both) in matters relating to employment or appointment to any office under the state.

2. No citizen shall on ground only of religion, race, caste, sex, descent, place of birth, residence or any of them be ineligible for or discriminated against in respect of any employment in office under the state.

In Article 17, it is provided that untouchability is abolished and to practises it in any form is forbidden. The enforcement of disability arising out of untouchability shall be an offence punishable in accordance with law. Side by side, Article 14 provides: "the state shall not deny to any person equality before law and equal protection of the laws within the territory of India."

Article 15 prohibits discrimination on grounds of religion, race, caste, sex or place of birth, their access to shops, public restaurants, hotels and places of public entertainment or the use of wells, tanks, bathing ghats, roads and places of public resort maintained wholly or partly out of state funds or dedicated to the use of general public. Article 16(4) provides that "nothing in this article shall prevent the state from making any provision for reservation of appointments or post in favour of any backward class of citizens, which in the opinion of the state, is not adequately represented in the services under the State."

Of late, it has been observed that the use of this clause in Uttar Pradesh has invited lots of criticism from a section of society. But then is it wrong, if one is in power and uses the clauses in favour of those who in return may be of some service to him? However, this is not a matter of inquiry. The focus is on who contributed to the introduction of the above provisions in the Constitution of India with great foresight and vision. He was, no doubt, Ambedkar whose battle for his own people brought him in great conflict with the view of many great national leaders. And Baba Saheb's energy was exhausted in avoiding sharp differences and confrontation with them. There were heated debates, walk-outs, compromises in the name of saving the life of the Father of the Nation but ultimately he succeeded in laying the foundation for the nation and for the coming generations to enjoy life as equals. No doubt, he was Ambedkar, and men and women belonging to the weaker sections cannot afford to forget him for generations to come. He was their true messiah. It will not be out of place to mention here that reservation was intended by the framers of the Constitution for a social purpose and that too exclusively for the socially and educationally backward classes, but, it is that which has been transformed into a socio-political purpose today.

Besides the quota fixed by Supreme Court of India at 50 per cent, several States have enhanced further or they are engaged in the process of enhancing it. Tamil Nadu has enhanced the reservation to 69 per cent and the Central Government, due to electoral constraint, accepted this hike. It was also agreed to amend the Constitution and include it in Ninth Schedule in order to place it beyond the purview of judicial review. Karnataka followed suit and enhanced it to 73 per cent and requested the centre to include it in Ninth Schedule. With this it is clear that the reservation issue has become out and out a political move. So long as reservation quotas, it is felt, serve political parties to retain power, nothing can be done to stop reservation's politicization. Perhaps the father of the Indian Constitution did not contemplate reservation to this extent. It becomes a complicated affair for judicial exercise. In one of his speeches, Ambedkar expressed the view that "we hold that the problem of depressed classes will never be solved unless they get political power in their own hands." But the exercise of the political power should be with reasonable restraints. It is said that if one consumes the whole apple or substantially the whole of it and leaves nothing or a little for others, it cannot be said to be fair at all. And for pleasing one class, it will displease the others. The Constitution makers permitted protective discrimination, but not without any reasonable limitation.[1]

The protective discrimination recognized by the provisions of the Constitution is largely concerned with certain classes of citizens of India who were regarded as sufferers or having suffered in the past from social and economic disabilities. Such classes of citizens are SCs, STs and OBCs. "Who are backward" has been interpreted by the courts from time to time but without a precise finality because some held the view that backwards were those who belonged to a particular caste, others were of the view that backward were those who were economically backward.[2]

Baba Saheb had sharp difference with Gandhi[3] who wanted uplift of all citizens, whereas Baba Saheb was more concerned with the uplift of backward classes. In one of his speeches,[4] he summed up his views on equality before law saying that we must begin by acknowledging the fact that two ills plague the Indian sociaty: a society based on the principle of graded inequality which means elevation for some and degradation for others, and on the other hand lie economic plane, we have a society and in which there are some who have immense wealth as against many who live in abject

1. P.M. Bakshi, "Reservation for Backward Classes — Some Reflections", in the *Journal of Indian Law Institute,* vol. 2, April-June, 1985, no. 2, p. 318.
2. *State of Andhra Pradesh* vs. Sagar, 1960 (3) SCR 595.
3. J.B. Kriplani, *Gandhi–His Life and Thought*, Government Publication, 1970.
4. *Constituent Assembly Debates*, 607-922 and 938-95.

poverty. On 26 January, we are going to enter into a life of contradictions. In politics, we will have equality and in social and economic life, we will have inequality. The condition of the untouchables, especially in rural areas, is still not good as it should have been.The SCs and STs (Prevention of Atrocities) Act, 1989 was enacted to achieve the goal enshrined in Article 17 of the Constitution. Article 17 of the Constitution abolishes untouchability and forbids its practice in any form. Article 17, it is observed in a practical application of the principle of equality before law and guarantees social justice as well as dignity to man. But instances are not lacking, where one comes across the fact that the practice has not yet ceased to exist in rural life. The cases of rape, loot, murder and different kinds of torture unknown to the cultured people have not been completely eliminated through legislation in many parts of the country. Why is it so? It remains a big unanswered question till date. This forces us to recall the note of warning once issued by Ambedkar that, if we were unable to remove contradictions at the earliest possible moment "those who suffered from inequality would blow up the structure of political democracy which that assembly had so laboriously built up." He further queried why India could not evolve a system of common brotherhood of all Indians, for "without fraternity, equality and liberty it will be no deeper than a coat of paint."[5]

It has been pointed out by Rajeev Dhawan in one of his articles that each part of the Constitution was subjected to some form of corruption in varying degrees. In one of his articles published in the vol. 36 no. I, 1994 (January—March) of Indian Law Institute pp. 8-9 under the heading: "Ambedkar's Prophecy-Poverty of Human Rights in India"—

5. Ibid., 979-80.

> The demand of the privileged dwarfed the struggles of the deprived, different people have put in their own words the pitiable state of affairs of the neglected lot. The poor are forced to fight and compete with each other. In the words of Baba Saheb, provisions contained in Parts III and IV of Indian Constitution were contradictory to each other as one was justifiable and the other was non-justifiable. One was provided and the other was to be provided in future. Was it not a case of gigantic Constitutional fraud? Of late, the courts have started giving significance to the provisions contained in Part IV of the Constitution. Article 39A of the Constitution of India provides that "the State shall secure that the operation of the legal system promotes justice on a basis of equal opportunity and shall in particular provide free legal aid by suitable legislation or schemes or in any other way, to ensure that opportunities of securing justice are not denied to any citizen by reason of economic or other disabilities.

Article 46 of the Constitution of India further provides that "the state shall promote with special care the educational and economic interests of the weaker sections of the people and in particular, of the SCs and STs and shall protect them from social injustice and all forms of exploitation." What is provided in the above articles still requires honest and true implementation in actual practice. However, the weaker sections' ability to secure free education, free legal aid, freedom from bonded labour and a life of grace and dignity is still a puzzling question. Who should look after their uplift — the government or the non governmental bodies. They suffer and will continue to suffer till women of the weaker sections of society do not get adequate Constitutional protection. There have been cases in which underprivileged women were paraded naked, raped publicly and put to shameful forms of torture at the hands of the privileged ones. Their homes were plundered and uprooted; belongings looted;

money robbed; innocent men, women and children subjected to inhuman conditions; and killed merely because they belonged to weaker sections of society. Nobody gives them real protection. The phrase "equality before law and equal protection of laws" does not instil confidence in the hearts of the poor and unprivileged lot. Because they are poor, they cannot afford to go to the Supreme Court. No advocate of repute having roaring practice willingly volunteers to give them legal aid. The Supreme Court of India is burdened with public interest litigations now. Can it on its own initiative do justice to the poor in all cases? One does not know the exact answer, because the concern for the betterment of the conditions of the weaker sections of society is not the concern of all yet. It is felt that the will to change the social set-up and fight the political rights of the privileged few has yet not gained that much momentum as it should have done. It is because of insincerity of people to do something positive for the poor or indifferent attitude towards them or a lethargic approach to the whole issue.

Ambedkar had been a revolutionary leader of the untouchables. He knew that his fight for his own people was not just with the State but with cruel forces in the Indian society itself.

Baba Saheb was the trusted and tested leader of the depressed classes. He was the saviour of the SCs. Who will now replace him and continue from where he left?

Justice Krishna Iyer in one of his articles "*Dynamics of Dissent*" has expressed the following view:

> Our goal is social justice underscored by the preambular pledge. Our task is to devise methods and modalities to redeem this Constitutional tryst even by dissent from *corpus juris* and the barbarities of ubiquitous corruption in high

> public life, oblique conduct of law-makers and law-dispensers. When the system keeps millions in sub-human status and millionaires in super-human control, practised inglorious grandeur and unconscienable brutality and jaundiced justice, when a nation becomes submissive and communal, feudal, medieval, and kilkenny cats, politically unmindful of the masses and the classes chase pleasure, position and shameless wealth, silence is a sin and dissent a duty . . . The explosive syndrome and passivist pathology are grave risks to our secular socialist republic. Then the therapeutic process of activist protest and functional dissent finds its finest hour of fulfilment. The day after is too late. Now-now to reduce disparity is the social goal of the Constitution."

Dr Ambedkar's views on the Weaker Sections of Society

Democracy is a mere cry in the wilderness in the absence of social equality.[6] The concept of democracy will be of no vital significance to the common man and woman of India unless it serves as means to bring about change in the socio-economic relations of the community to achieve the ideal of social equality. Thus social justice forms the signature tune of the Indian Constitution.[7] This founding faith has paramount position in our society because the struggle for freedom has been not only political but also economic and social. Gandhi, Nehru, Ambedkar and every other great Indian had visualized the imperatives of Independence as implying an integral approach. Ambedkar was emphatic that, "we make our political democracy." To Ambedkar, "democracy" refers to

---

6. B.R. Ambedkar, *The Report of the Backward Classes Commission*, vol. 3, 1956, pp. 73-75. We want that all communities should come up to the same level and one class should have the same respect for the other as the other class has got for it.
7. *Constituent Assembly Debates*, 25-11-1949, vol. 11, p. 972.

fundamental changes in the social and economic life of the people and acceptance of those changes by the people without resorting to disputes and bloodshed.[8]

Painfully conscious of the social and economic inequalities which corroded the national consciousness of the Indian people, he unrelentingly desired to remove the contradictions created by economic and social inequalities. He wanted to establish the principles of one-man-one-vote and one-vote-one-value not only in the political life of India but also in its social and economic spheres.[9] He firmly believed that,

> the first condition which I think precedent for the successful working of democracy is that there must be no glaring inequalities in the society. There must not be an oppressed class and there must not be a suppressed class. There must not be a class which has got all the privileges and a class which has got all the burdens to carry. Such a thing, such a division, such an organization of society has within itself the germs of a bloody revolution and perhaps it would be impossible for democracy to cure them.[10] The aim to get India out of the medievalism based on birth, religion, community and custom and reconstruct her social structure on rational foundation of law, individual merit and secular education could be effected only through such provisions which contain protective and compensatory discrimination to recognize the factual existence of backwardness in our country brought about by historical reasons coupled with

---

8. Ambedkar in a speech delivered before the members of the Poona District Law Library on 22-12-1952. Quoted in *Ambedkar's College Magazine*, Mahad, 1962.
9. Ambedkar in a speech on "Conditions Precedent for the Successful Working of Democracy in Poona" quoted in *Ambedkar's College Magazine*, Mahad, 1962.
10. V.R. Krishna Iyer, *Social Justice, Sunset Dawn*, 2nd edn., 1987, p. 5.

> sincere attempts to promote the welfare of the weaker sections thereof. Accordingly, the Constituent Assembly, when it set its final seal on the National Charter, did hearken to the holistic nature of social, economic and political equality if democracy were to be stable. The explosive pervasiveness of appalling economic deprivations and social suppressions made this keynote thought the most profound ideology of the Constitution. Thus, it came to be realized that democracy is not only a form of life but also a form of life through which social justice can be established. Social justice demands that society should promote the welfare of all and not merely the happiness of the greatest number.

Modern concept of social equality consists in the spirit to uplift the downtrodden, to console the frustrated, to raise the suppressed, to advance the backward and to protect the weaker sections of the society. Social equality consists in bringing up on par those whose levels of consciousness have been low either by tradition or by treatment. In this context, the reference to the weaker sections of the society is to the weakness arising out of their status as women, as religious minorities, as member of SCs and STs or OBCs — a status essentially imposed by birth over which they have no control. Hence, it is proposed in this chapter to make a study of the improvement of the biologically weak, viz. women, and the socially weak, viz. the down-trodden classes, sought to be made by the singular efforts of the great social reformer, Bhimrao Ramji Ambedkar.

As Justice V.R. Krishna Iyer opines,

> Communalism and religious fanaticism are invasions on social justice, especially gender justice, because our gods are masculine as professed by fundamentalists of every faith. Wearing the holy visage of Manu and Mohammad, Jesus and Zoroaster, these exploitative forces use theology

> of human rights. The biggest minority in India is its womanhood subjected to generations of gender injustice.
>
> The system of joint family and the self-enclosed village perpetuated the caste system and allied superstitious social customs. The social reform postulated by Ambedkar was double-pronged: one, the reform of the Hindu family and the other, the reorganization and reconstruction of the Hindu society. The problems of *sati*, widow re-marriage, child marriage, etc. relate to the social reform of the Hindu family while the abolition of the caste system, abolition of untouchability, changes in the law of marriage, adoption and succession relate to the social reform in the larger sense of the reorganization and reconstruction of the Hindu society.[11]

A thorough study of the *Manusmriti* helped Ambedkar to realize that women were looked upon as objects for seducing men,[12] able to lead astray in (this) world not only a fool, but even a learned man, and to make him a slave of desire and anger[13] and hence it was enjoined upon men to strenuously exert themselves to guard woman,[14] knowing their disposition — love of ornament, impure desires, wrath, dishonesty, malice, and bad conduct — which the Lord of Creatures laid in them at the creation to be such.[15] Consequently, day and night women must be kept in dependence by the males of

---

11. G.H. Lokhande, *Bhimrao Ramji Ambedkar : A Study in Social Democracy*, 1982, p. 143.
12. Vide *Manusmriti*, II.213: "It is the nature of women to seduce man in this world; for that reason the wise are never unguarded in the company of females."
13. Ibid. II.214: "For woman are able to lead astray in this world not only a fool, but even a learned man, and (to make) him a slave of desire and hunger."
14. Ibid., IX. 17.
15. Ibid., IX. 2.

their families and if they attach themselves to sexual enjoyments, they must be kept under one's control. They needed to be controlled vigilantly by their guardian. They did not have the right to divorce. A wife was reduced by Manu to the level of a slave in the matter of property. She was also subjected to corporal punishment as the husband had the right to beat his wife. Women did not have choice in selecting a spouse. The father had the right to settle the marriage of his daughter. She had to worship her husband faithfully even if he be a debauch or a man devoid of virtues and other human qualities.[16] Manu made another new rule which stated that killing a woman was only a *upapataka,* that it was only a minor offence.[17]

Thus, Ambedkar arrived at the conclusion:

> . . . can anybody doubt that it was Manu who was responsible for the degradation of woman in India? Most people are perhaps aware of this. But they do not seem to know two facts. They do not know what is peculiar to Manu. There is nothing new or startling in the laws of Manu about woman. They are the views of the Brahmins ever since Brahmanism was born in India. Before Manu they existed only as a matter of social theory. What Manu did was to convert which was a social theory into the law of the State.

---

16. Vide, *Encyclopedia Britannica*: "The very word women etymologically meaning a wife, sums up the long history of dependence and subordination." Also, compare Gibbon's statement quoted in M.H. Sheikh Kidwai, *Women under Different Social and Religious Laws*, 1976, p. 3, "such was the stern and haughty spirit of the ancient law that women were condemned to the perpetual tutelage of priests, husbands or guardians: a sex created to please and to obey was never supposed to have attained the age of reason and experience."
17. Supra, note 10, pp. XI, 67.

> The second thing they do not know is the reason which led Manu to impose these disabilities upon women. Shudras and women were the two chief sections of the Aryan society which were flocking to join the religion of the Buddha and thereby undermining the foundation of Brahmanic religion. Manu wanted to stem the tide of women following in the direction of Buddhism.[18]

No doubt,

> women from the point of view of sex and femininity are the same all over the world but surely it cannot be said that the women of all over the world share the affection of their husbands with their rivals or that they are married when they are in their cradle or when they are children. Therefore, what led to this discrimination in this country is not the fact that women had a sex different from men, but that women in this country were so situated that special legislation was required in order to protect them.[19] Fully conscious of the need to uplift the status of women, while speaking on the Hindu Code Bill in the Constituent Assembly, he stressed the need to have a common code which could do away with the rules of Hindu law scattered in innumerable decisions of the High Courts, and of the Privy Council, on seven different matters that is: (1) the right to property of a deceased female and male, (2) the order of succession among the different heirs to the property of a deceased dying intestate; (3) the law of maintenance; (4) marriage, (5) divorce, (6) adoption, and (7) minority and guardianship.[20]

The striking feature of the Hindu Code Bill was that it was a wonderful fusion of the orthodox and modern approaches.

---

18. B.R. Ambedkar, *The Rise and Fall of the Hindu Woman*, 1965, p. 24.
19. Per Chagla C.J. in *Yusuf* vs. *State of Bombay, A.I.R.*, 1951 Bombay, 471.
20. B.R. Ambedkar, *Case for Hindu Code*, 1949, pp. 12-37.

Thus, in matters of marriage, a Hindu could choose either to follow the old Shastric rules and choose his marital spouse from the same *varna* or could choose to be a reformist and marry outside his community. Both types of marriages were valid. Drawing support from historical precedents,[21] he was confident that the introduction of the law of monogamy as an inviolable rule would not receive the wrath of criticism of the general public. Similarly, the provisions in *Naradsmriti* and *Parasharasmriti* permitting a woman to take a second husband enabled him to introduce the concept of divorce in Hindu matrimonial law.

Under the Hindu Code Bill,[22] in matters relating to adoption, secular principles, viz. adopting of a child from any community of one's choice, validity of adoption of a female child or orphan child either by an unmarried Hindu male or female were introduced. Further, the rule of divesting of property from the Hindu widow by an adopted son was sought to be done away with. He writes,

> "I do not understand why there should be adoption. Most of us who make adoptions have no name to be recorded in

21. Monogamous marriages were the rule at the time of Kautilya. Only when the husband was convinced that the wife was barren after cohabiting with her for 10-15 years, and on his return to the wife all the *stridhana* acquired by her at the time of marriage, was the husband free to have a second marriage. Similarly, under the Aliasantans system, monogamy was the prescribed rule of marital life.

22. The story of the Hindu Code Bill and its success is told with very succinct comment by T.P. Gopal Krishna et al., *Codified Hindu Laws,* Allahabad, 1960, pp. 1-75. For a detailed study also refer V. Suryanarayan Rao, *Women under Hindu Law (Need for Reform)*, Madras (1941), V.S. Srinivasa Sastri, *Rights and Status of Women in India,* Madras (1956) and Derrett, *A Critique of Modern Hindu Law,* Bombay (1970).

> history, because my record is probably very poor. I am an unusual member of the Hindu community. But there are many who have no record to go down and I do not understand why they should indulge in adopting a son, a stupid body, uneducated, without any character, not knowing his possibilities and fastening himself upon a poor woman, whom he can deprive of every property that she possessed. Therefore my idea is this, that if you do not want to cherish your old notions with regard to adoptions at any rate make this provision that the adopted boy does not deprive the mother of the property which is her mainstay. I do not think, that limitation can be at all a point of controversy.[23]

However, the Hindu Code Bill though drafted with the best motives was stiffly opposed by many orthodox members of Parliament. Shyama Prasad Mookerji said that the Hindu Code Bill would shatter the magnificent structure of Hindu culture and stultify a dynamic and catholic way of life that had wonderfully adapted itself to the changes for centuries. Sardar Bhopendra Singh Mann termed the code a conversion law. However, others like N.V. Gadgil and Pandit Kunzru openly supported the bill and the woman members described the Bill as a testament of their faith in the Constitution.[24]

The Hindu Code Bill was not the outcome of a delirious mind antithetic to anything and everything relating to Hinduism and containing preposterous and outrageous provisions totally alien to the Hindu culture and way of life. The committee consisting of Justice B.N. Rau (Chairman), Dwarakanath Mitter, Principal J.R. Charpure and T.R. Venkatarama Shastri toured around important places in the

---

23. Supra, note 19, p. 34.
24. Dhananjay Keer, *Ambedkar — Life and Mission*, Popular Prakashan, Bombay, 1971, pp. 432-33.

country, sent out a questionnaire to all important persons interested in the study of Hindu law, examined a large number of these persons orally, considered the replies sent by them and finally presented their report along with a draft of the Bill to amend and codify certain branches of the Hindu law. The report was reviewed by a selected committee and the Hindu Code as it was originally placed before the Indian Parliament had thus evolved after considerable consultation and in-depth study. Besides, the original draft underwent many modifications following the amendments suggested by the members. The committee on the Hindu Code, the Select Committee of the Parliament and the Law Minister, B.R. Ambedkar carefully scrutinized all the provisions of the draft and gave it proper shape and form. Hence, it was with a deep sense of anguish that Ambedkar writes:

> they will realize that this is in no sense a revolutionary measure. I say that this is not even a radical measure. If these people (B.N. Rau Committee), conservative in their attitude have signed the report, I think we can take it for granted that the measure to which they have put their signatures could not be revolutionary and certainly would not be destructive of the foundations of the Hindu society. So far as I am concerned, I am a very conservative person. Although some people may not accept that fact, I am indeed very conservative. All I say is that I am a progressive conservative.[25]

No wonder, Justice Gajendragadkar, a famous jurist and Sanskrit scholar opined:

> If with the active co-operation and support of the Prime Minister, who fortunately shares his Law Minister's enthusiasm for the Code, Ambedkar is able to pilot the Code through all the stages and give it the pride of place in our

25. Supra, note 19, p. 34.

> Statute Book, I for one would hail it as time's sweet revenge on the Hindu society as a whole. If Ambedkar gives us Hindus our Code, his achievement would go down in history as a very eloquent piece of poetic justice indeed.[26]

However, the Bill was let down in a tragic manner — "it was killed and buried unwept and unused after four clauses were passed. Now, his vision of a reformed Hindu law was totally blurred, with disappointment and frustration that his fervent desire had become wholly futile. Ambedkar resigned his seat from the Cabinet itself, "For a long time I have been thinking of resigning my seat from the Cabinet," he wrote. "The only thing that had held me back from giving effect to my intention was the hope that it would be possible to give effect to the Hindu Code Bill before the life of the present Parliament came to an end. I even agreed to break up the Bill and restrict it to Marriage and Divorce in the hope that at least this much of our labour may bear fruit. But even part of the Bill has been killed, I see no purpose in my continuing to be member of your cabinet."[27]

Though Ambedkar left office "bereft of the crown of Manu," with passage of time, not only the reformists but also the conservatives found it obligatory to lend their support to it. Thus, H.V. Pataskar went down in history as the person responsible for re-introducing the truncated Hindu Code Bill. Thus, the Hindu Code suppressed the customs recognized by nearly 137 *Smritis* including the *Smritis* of *Manu* and *Yajnavalkya* and also the precedents of the Privy Council which recognized that custom is transcendent law and overrides the written law. Through the laudable efforts of the modern Manu, the

26. Justice Gajendragadkar, "The Hindu Code Bill," Lectures delivered before the students of Karnatak University, Dharwar, 1951, p. 26.

27. Supra, note 23, p. 352.

centuries-old injustice inflicted on women providing them with only one-fourth share in the father's property, and inability to either adopt or to be adopted has been completely abrogated and the rightful place for women with equal shares and absolute rights in property matters and equal rights in all share of personal law have now been given. The realization, appreciation and recognition of the important role that women should be duly accorded in any civilized society came naturally to a person who was firmly engaged in the struggle for reclamation of human personality forced by the stratified Hindu society to live a life of surrender, servitude and helplessness. Ambedkar was a believer, in women's organizations.[28] He knew that they would do to improve society if they were convinced. In the eradication of social evils they had rendered great services. He measured the progress of a community by the degree of progress which women had achieved. He had advised women, "learn to be clean, keep away from vices . . ., give education to your children. Instil ambition into them. Inculcate in their minds that they are destined to be great, remove from them all inferiority complex. Do not be in a hurry to marry. Marriage is a liability. You should not impose it upon your children unless they are financially able to meet the liabilities arising from marriage. Those who marry will have to keep in mind that to have too many children is a crime. The paternal duty lies in giving each child a better start than its parent had, above all, let every girl who marries stand by her husband, claim to be her husband's friend and equal and refuse to be his slave. I am sure if you follow this advice, you will bring honour and glory to yourselves," he concluded. The essence of his mission was to uplift the status of weaker sections, viz. women and the

28. Ibid.

depressed classes and was focused on the exhortation to the Hindus to reconstruct the society to suit the needs of time. He explained, "those who want to conserve must be ready to repair and all I want is that if you want to maintain the Hindu system, the Hindu culture, the Hindu's society, do not hesitate to repair where it is necessary."[29]

Now,[30] in the 1990s, if women are able to leave the confines of their homes in pursuit of education or career; they are able to compete in all fields of life shoulder to shoulder with men; approach the courts for redressal of matrimonial problems from fraud to insanity to option of puberty to cruelty; adopt any child of their choice in their own right; hold property as absolute owners with equal rights as their male counterparts, and thus be treated as equals on par with men; the whole credit goes exclusively to the modern Manu, Ambedkar. Hindu women are greatly indebted to this great scholar for their redemption from bondage and complete subjugation under male tyranny sanctioned by pseudo-religious injunctions.

A detailed study of his life and mission reveals that Ambedkar held the grund norm, the basic or fundamental norm, to be equality — social, economic and political — from which he proceeded to lay down a collection of "ought" propositions; in this hierarchy of "oughts," the initial fundamental "ought" on which the validity of all the other ultimately rests, the grund norm seems to be social equality,

---

29. Ibid., p. 41.

30. On women in modern India, see: *Towards Equality, Report of the Committee on the Status of Women in India*, Department of Social Welfare, Ministry of Education and Social Welfare, Government of India, Delhi, 1974; P. Kapur, *The Changing Status of the Working Women in India*, New Delhi, 1974; and B.R. Nanda, ed., *Indian Women–From Purdah to Modernity*, New Delhi, 1976.

the justification for the rest of the legal reforms and changes he so assiduously fought for. Naturally with exposure to both the rigid Hindu philosophy emphasizing the stratified social inequality based on birth as the norm and the liberal egalitarian Western philosophy, he was supremely conscious of his mission in life, which was essentially to strive for reforms aiming at annihilation of exploitation and social inequality and also guaranteeing to each member of society complete and manifold development of all his (physical, material and spiritual) creative forces and ensuring true human freedom and personal independence.

Born as an untouchable, Ambedkar had to face social ostracism and contemptuous degrading treatment. That very early experience in life made him conscious of the unwarranted inequality imposed on Hindus by caste Hindus in the name of religion.[31] He felt that the Hindu society lacked social endosmosis. The caste system sanctified by the pernicious ideal of *chaturvarna* perpetuated the practice of endogamy which widened the chasm between the various segments of society. The Hindu society, he believed, needed a wholesome radical change. Instead of blaming a man, for the religious customs observed by him, which would have been a futile exercise, he adopted the wise course of educating society in the principles and values of democracy. To agitate for and to organize inter-caste dinners and inter-caste marriages is like force-feeding brought about by artificial means. Make every man and woman free from the thralldom of the Shastras, cleanse their minds of the pernicious notions founded on the Shastras, and

31. Vide, Ambedkar's words in supra, note 23, p. 468. "If I fail to do away with abominable thraldom and human injustice under which the class to which I belong has been groaning, I will put an end to my life with a bullet."

encourage him/her to do so. His slogan, "tell the slave that he is a slave and he will revolt against his slavery and fight for his self-respect and his self-devotion." Until this clarion call, the untouchables were dormant politically, economically and socially[32] though they were well aware of the inhuman hardships and humiliations and indignities imposed on them by caste Hindus. They were led to believe and were convinced that the present situation was because of their previous lives. Hence it is not strange that Ambedkar expressed his anguish to the depressed classes thus:[33]

> My heart breaks to see the pitiable sight of your faces and to hear your sad voices. You have been groaning from time immemorial and yet you are not ashamed to hug your helplessness as inevitability. Why did you not perish in the pre-natal stage instead? Why do you worsen and sadden the picture of the sorrows, poverty, slavery and burdens of the world with your deplorable, despicable, detestable and miserable life? You had better died and relieved this world if you could not rise to a new life and if you could not rejuvenate yourself. As a matter of fact, it is your birthright to get food, shelter and clothing in equal proportion with every individual, high or low. If you believe in living a respectable life you should believe in self-help which is the best help.

He tried to goad his people into action citing the examples of France and the emancipation of Negroes from slavery, "we are demanding equal rights which are the common possession of the entire humanity but due to inhibitions created by the Shastras we have been denied these human rights. I am telling you that wherever human rights were snatched away, there, battles and wars were fought and bloodshed was witnessed.

32. B.R. Ambedkar, *Anihilation of Caste*, p. 75.
33. Supra, note 23, pp. 60-61.

In case of France, when the nobles denied the human rights to the lower class people, they massacred the nobles until they finally won the battle. The battle was continued for more than ten years. In America too, the American people fought the civil war in order to emancipate the Negroes from slavery. In the civil war, those who died did so after doing certain noble deeds. Those who remained alive enjoyed the happiness of free men. Such a kind of battle was required in order to restitute the lost human rights. But I do not understand how our people, even though they were put to injustice, mortification and insult could still tolerate them like a dumb lot of humanity and like a submissive cow. We never feel sorry, we never get annoyed and we never realize the insults.

"We are self-satisfied, even though we have been kicked by the caste-Hindu people. What are the reasons which made us dead in mentality and spirit? I find we don't have economic, social and physical strength. Whoever has knowledge, wisdom and strength is capable of tyrannizing those who do not have any of them. Therefore, the particular code of conduct was assigned to us by those who had the knowledge, wisdom and strength. I am very sorry to say that because of the ignorance, gullibility and utter submissiveness, we are suffering this injustice. As we are not conscious of the heritage acquired by the humanity we made our position deplorable, helpless and therefore, we are facing the difficulties of food, clothing and the place of shelter even though India is a country which is called a golden country. In the midst of plenty, we are poverty-stricken. I, therefore, give you the clarion call that you should not be self-satisfied, self-complacent and be the worshipper of the old value. I do not want that whatever our ancestors did, the ancestral deeds, we should do the same thing. We have to change the present situation, When we change the present situation I am sure, the code of conduct forced on us will be quite impossible for us to fight against the odd circumstances. Don't believe in accidents and coincidence. Believe that man is the creator of history and he can come out successful, notwithstanding the odd circumstances."[34]

Apart from what have already been stated, he started educational and social institutions and journals and also launched a movement, *satyagraha,* for the steady and systematic uplift of the downtrodden. On 9 March 1924, at the Damodhar Hall, Bombay, he called a meeting of social workers and established the Bahiskrit Hitkarini Sabha mainly:

a. to promote the spread of education among the depressed classes by opening hostels and by employing such other means as may seem necessary or desirable;

b. to promote the spread of culture among the depressed classes by opening libraries, social centres and classes or study circles;

c. to advance and improve the economic condition of the depressed classes by starting industrial and agricultural schools; and

d. to represent the grievances of the depressed class.[35] Thus, through the Bahiskarit Hitkarini Sabha, he started high schools and hostels for the untouchables. He then established the Bhartiya Bahiskrit Samaj Seva Sangh, the motto of which was "read, read out and hear; understand, realize and give realization."[36]

This *modus operandi* adopted by Ambedkar won him enviable popularity owing to his pragmatic approach. He also staged a

34. Shankarrao Kharat, ed., *Letters of Babasaheb Ambedkar* Marathi edn., pp. 11-13.

35. Supra, note 23, pp. 54-55.

36. Supra, note I, p. 173.

satyagraha at Mahad to seek permission for the untouchables to take water from the "Chavdar" lake. *Bahishkrit Bharat*, a fortnightly, was started by Ambedkar in 1927. He kept himself busy with conferences and meetings where he gave his plans and schemes to the untouchables. In 1936, he formed the Independent Labour Party. The party in its manifesto combined economic and social programmes. Seeing that the party was not serving the purpose for which it was established, it was transformed into Scheduled Caste Federation.

Ambedkar put pressure on the caste Hindus to bury age-old tradition founded on inequality. The caste Hindus had to take note of his demand because "his demand was not that of a beggar but that of a person robbed of his rights."[37] Since he confined himself to the uplift of the untouchables only, he could mobilize them with greater ease.

The problems of the untouchables had been broached upon earlier too. The Montague–Chelmsford Report made certain recommendations for safeguarding their special interest. But the recommendations were petty and did not touch the core of the problem. The first Round Table Conference was given a memorandum by Ambedkar which covered adequate representation of the depressed classes in legislatures, measures against boycott or threat of boycott, protection against discrimination, adequate reservation in services, right to redressal against prejudicial action, or neglecting their interests, formation of special department for taking care of the untouchables and representation in the Cabinet.[38]

The Government Declaration of 1932 regarding communal representation recognized separate constituencies for the

---

37. A.K. Vakil, *Reservation Policy and Scheduled Castes in India*, 1985, p. 10.
38. Ibid., p. 3.

depressed classes but gave them two votes—one for community candidate and another for general candidate. However, as this decision of Ramsay MacDonald, the then British minister, caused resentment and enmity amidst the upper caste Hindu politicians, it came to be realized by Ambedkar that it was imperative to embody certain safeguards for the depressed classes in the Constitution itself. It was to be done through guarantee of minimum representation to them in legislatures, executive and administrative services.

Ambedkar knew it all well and therefore he constantly fought for Constitutional safeguards.[39] (Their representation was to be made on the basis of their population. Ambedkar preferred a separate electorate for the untouchables. Concerning the (definition of the Scheduled Caste Order, 1936, under the Government of India Act, 1935 should be used.)

Ambedkar, a leader of the depressed classes, was Chairman of the Constitution Draft Committee, a rare honour indeed. The objective resolution moved by Pandit Nehru, which later on approximately formed the text of the Preamble, guaranteed justice as regards economic, political, social fields and safeguards for the SCs, STs and OBCs in India.

The provisions for equality in the Constitution legally removed social and political restrictions on the SCs and STs, and the privileges enabled them to come up to the standards of the other citizens of India.[40] Article 14 — equality before law — legally wiped off the injustice done to the weaker and depressed classes. It further implied removal of discrimination regulated by the arrangement implicit in the conception of

39. Ibid., p. 7.

40. Cf. "The Liberal Paradigm of Affirmative Action Conceptualized by Rawls in Theory of Justice, 1971" p. 73, In the System of Natural Liberty the Initial Distribution:

careers open to talents in which positions are open to those able and willing to strive for them. These arrangements presuppose a background of equal liberty and free market economy. They require a formal equality of opportunity in that all have at least the same legal rights of access to all advantaged social positions. But since there is no effort to preserve an equality or similarity of social conditions, except insofar as this is necessary to preserve the requisite background institutions, the initial distribution of assets for any period of time is strongly influenced by natural and social contingencies. The existing distribution of natural assets — that is, natural talents and abilities — as these have been developed or left unrealized, and their use favoured or disfavoured over time by social circumstances and such chance non-cogencies as accident and good fortune. The liberal interpretation . . . tries to correct for this by addition to requirement of careers open to talents the further condition of the principle of fair equality of opportunity. Though here is that position is to be not only open in a formal sense but that all should have a fair chance to attain them . . . assuming as that there is a distribution of natural assets, those who are at the same level of talent and ability and have the same willingness to use them, should have the same prospects of success regardless of their initial place in the social systems the liberal interpretation . . . seek . . . to mitigate the influence of social contingencies and natural fortune on distributive shares."

Free access by all citizens of India regardless of caste, sect, sex, etc. to public places, shops, hotels, restaurants and places of entertainment was ensured. The use of wells, roads, bathing ghats, tanks, etc. was thrown open to all. "This provision in the Constitution is really revolutionary."[41]

---

41. Supra, note 37, p. 18.

The attempt to secure equality goes beyond guarantee of equal treatment by government. The crucial provisions regulate not only "state action" but also the behaviour of private persons and groups. Caste discrimination by government or private individuals is banned. But it was recognized that even-handed treatment would not suffice to overcome the cumulative disadvantages of those at the bottom of the social hierarchy. To promote the advancement of the untouchables, tribals and other socially and educationally backward classes, the Constitution allows protective or compensatory discrimination on their behalf.[42] The notion of communal quotas and safeguards which had become an accepted and prominent principle of administration during the last forty years of the British rule was decisively rejected as a general principle of governance. There are no safeguards for religious minorities apart from the guaranteed fundamental rights. Only for the SCs and STs (and to a lesser extent, for OBCs) are these devices countenanced. There is a deliberate departure from formal norms of equality in order to offset the historic inequalities of these groups.[43] Ambedkar explained:

> "Although, theoretically it is good to have the principle that there shall be equality of opportunity, there must at the same time be a provision made for the entry of certain communities which have so far been outside the administration."[44]

---

42. Vide, K.M. Munshi, *Constituent Assembly Debates*, vol. X, p. 261."Except backward classes who are economically and socially backward, and the scheduled castes and tribes who have a special claim of their own, no other minority should be recognized in the Constitution."

43. Marc Galanter, *Competing Equalities–Law and the Backward Classes in India*, 1984, pp. 38-39.

44. *Constituent Assembly Debates*, vol. III, p. 701, Also compare the opinion of Ratna Revankar in the Indian Constitution. *A Case Study of Backward Classes*, p. 50, "It is quite appropriate

Thus, compensatory discrimination programmes are authorized by Constitutional provisions (viz. Article 46, Article 16[4], Article 15[4]) which permit departure from formal equality for the purpose of favouring specified groups.[45] It was essential to simultaneously grant the depressed classes various facilities if political democracy is to be meaningful.

The benefits of "Compensatory discrimination" are extended to three major classes. First, there are the castes designated as SCs on the basis of untouchability. Second, there are the STs who are distinguished by their tribal culture and physical isolation and many of whom are residents of specially protected scheduled areas. Third, there are OBCs, a heterogeneous category, varying greatly from state to state, composed for the most part of castes (and some non-Hindu communities) low in the traditional social hierarchy, and a few tribal and nomadic groups as well as converts to non-Hindu religions from the SCs and in some areas the denotified tribes.

Preference is extended on a communal basis and basically can be grouped into three types: reservations which allot or facilitate access to valued positions or resources, e.g. reserved seats in legislatures,[46] reservation of posts in government

→ that the Backward Classes should look to the Constitution for special favours to redress the wrongs done in the past by creating social disabilities. It is equally justifiable that the Constitution should make special provisions to safeguard the interests of backward classes."

45. Vide, Mohd. Ghouse, *"Judicial Control of Protective Discrimination,"* 11 J.I.L.I. 371 (1969): "A society is as strong as its weakest sections. Therefore, to protect and promote interests of such sections is to stabilize and strengthen the society."

46. But T.N. Shalla attributes the following glaring defects to the existing system of legislative reservations: (1) It has failed →

→ to send genuine representatives from these scheduled groups to the Legislature. It has been found that those who get elected on these reserved seats are mere "appendages" and "shadows" congenial to the dominant political parties. They belong more to these dominant parties than to their groups. (2) The gap between these members and their group population is much wider. Further, a person once elected to the legislature tries to settle near the seat of power and away from his original moorings. (3) Among the scheduled groups only those politically conscious dominant benefit from the scheme. (4) The scheme has not helped the growth of political groupings and parties among the scheduled groups. Their political leaders have chosen the strategy of working with and through the well-established political parties. In their quest for personal gains, they seem to have lost their bargaining power. In such a situation they are unable to ensure effective implementation of any ameliorative policy or programme for their people. (5) Effectiveness of the legislative reservations has been greatly reduced by the abolition of double-member constituency in 1961. It has been found that reservation made some sense when there was plurality of seats. (6) The policy of legislative reservations has an opiate effect, it puts to sleep the instinct for social justice and dynamism that should come from an under-privileged class. "T.N. Shalla, Dynamics of Reservation Policy under Indian Constitution: A Working Paper" in D.N. Saraf (ed.), *Social Policy, Law and Protection of Weaker Sections of Society* (1986), p. 122. Vide, the observation of Khanna J. in *State of Kerala* vs. *N.M Thomas* (1976) S.C.C., 310-401 that an authorization of preferential treatment under Article 16(1) would vest the state, under the garb of classification, with power of treating sections of population as favoured classes of citizens for public employment. Article 16(2) may also not prove very effective, because the prohibitions contained therein may be circumscribed by mentioning grounds other than those specified in the clause. If inroads were allowed into the quality concept beyond those permissible under Article 16(4), the "ideals of supremacy of merit, the efficiency of services and the absence →

service,[47] and, besides reservation of places in academic institutions,[48] the allotment of land, housing and other resources;[49] programmes involving expenditure or provisions of services, e.g. scholarships, grants, loans, health care, legal aid; and special protection (e.g. Article 17).[50]

Dr Ambedkar, "the harbinger of social renaissance in India"was the mastermind behind this silent revolution[51] which

---

→ of discrimination in the sphere of public employment would be the obvious casualties." Also see the observation of V.R. Krishna Iyer in the same case: "You cannot throw to the winds considerations of administrative capability and grind the wheels of government to a halt in the name of *harijan welfare.*" Administration runs for good government; not to give jobs to harijans. *A.I.R.* 1976 SC 490, 526.

47. In his address to the 71st Meeting of the Inter-State Board for Anglo-Indian Education, Frank Anthony focused the attention of the educationists to consider the disastrous consequences of the politically inspired policy of reservations for the SCs and STs and OBCs in educational institutions to the virtual exclusion of others who are becoming the "new untouchables." cited in supra, note 46, p. 131.

48. Cf. Mohd. Ghouse, Supra note 45, p. 377:

    In our caste-ridden society, the caste-oriented behaviour of the vote has led to the emergence of political parties banking on caste-communalism. Such parties, under strong pressure from their voters, will confer special privileges and benefits on those who may not even need them."

49. Supra, note 43, pp. 42-43.

50. As described by Laxmanshastri Joshi, *Tarakateertha Asmila Dasha* Marathi Quarterly, Diwali Special Issue (1973).

51. Compare the view of S. Radhakrishnan, who — referring to socio—economic justice contemplated in the Objectives Resolution — said that "it intended to effect a smooth and rapid transition from a state of serfdom to one of freedom." Constituent Assembly Debates, vols. II, III, p. 253.

is now unfolding itself with all its beneficial effects of increasing social solidarity in Indian life.[52]

But there is still a long way to go. The cretinous influence of an iniquitous social order eulogistically designated as the oldest civilization cannot be got rid of within the short span of a few decades howsoever earnest be the efforts in that direction.[53] The whole philosophy of social equality as enshrined in our Constitution aims at converting the obscurantist and traditional Indian mind into a modern rational mind. Our community must be exposed to the realities of modern democratic liberalism and must learn to live on the basis of absolute social equality and regulate our relations purely by reason. But the message of social justice based on rationality must be strenuously practised and carried not only to big places, but also to small hamlets and this task must be attempted consistently and persistently until it dispels the obscurantist mist.[54] It is the responsibility of the new generation of enlightened men and women to carry forward the mission of Ambedkar with renewed vigour and determination. Let us erase in free India the man-made barriers carved in the name of caste, creed, social status or sex.[55] Let us practise a pragmatic style of learning, respecting and giving each and every Indian citizen his or her due share of equality. As it has been succinctly put:

---

52. Supra, note 9, p. 250.
53. Ibid., p. 234.
54. Supra, note 2, p. 223.
55. Vide, the definition of social justice given by Indira Gandhi in her address on 14th January 1974, "Social Justice in India means not only removing economic disparity as between classes but also the wiping out of social discrimination and disabilities. Our social revolution is a frontal attack on castes."

> What we need today is one single caste of humanity, one common religion of love and one universal language of the heart. No society can find its fulfilment, no social ideal can fructify without the blossoming of the spirit of man.[56]

56. Sri Satya Sai Baba, *Sanathan Sarathi*, Prasanthi Nilayam, Anantpur, vol. 21 : 3, p. 64 (May, 1978).

7

Linguistic Inquiries as to the Meaning of Justice

PHILOLOGISTS and philosophers in the last fifty years have paid increasing attention to the study of semantics — particularly, descriptive semantics (meaning of given words at a given time).[1] But, whereas the philosophers abandoned their emphasis on what is the meaning of words and concentrated on the use of words, the question for the philologists have persisted: "what is the function of this word in the typical utterances in which we employ it?"[2] In the present context linguistic inquiry is primarily concerned with the function which is served by the utterances containing the word "justice." But the contribution of linguistic analysis is dispiritingly small and dangerously unreliable. One writer has recently concluded on the basic of usage that we readily apply "fair" in the context of a process and we tend to reserve "justice" for use with reference to outcomes alone, and that as between the two elements of equality and reciprocity, "justice" tends to be appropriated especially to the former, and fairness to the latter.[3] But Allen warns that there is "scarcely a single relationship of life into which the question of justice does not

1. S. Willman, *The Principles of Semantics*, 2nd edn., 1957, p. 36.

2. See, Hart, *The Concept of Law.*

3. See, J. Chapman, *Justice and Fairness*, pp. 154-63.

enter."[4] Therefore, while we set some limit by fiat this must not be arbitrary. The word "justice" provides us with a warrant to exclude such uses: "just" as in "just a moment," "just here," "just right," and as we have "just said," for in all these cases the word "just" may be replaced by some paraphrase or circumlocution without any change in meaning. Similarly we may exclude such usage as: "he complained with justice," "a just observation" and "just indignation" and a host of usages such as "to do justice," "there is no justice in this law," "a just man," "a just conduct," "a just punishment," "a just law," "a just price" and "a just reward," Sciour, of a norm or of value, justice' refers to a social situation — social justice.[5]

Justice in Theory — A Normative Component of Social Action

The idea behind theory of justice is to give a degree of rational structuring to our ideas of justice. According to C.J. Friedrich, "Justice is never given, it is always a task to be achieved. Its incomplete realization does not result from the criteria, but from their fluidity. It is not the right word either, for it is the steady evolution and devolution of values which cause the difficulty."[6] The sociological jurist has, among his tasks, the study of the formation of ideas of justice and their impact on law and society. Even theories of analytical jurisprudence often proceed on assumptions about justice and processing the materials requisite for doing justice. There is multifariousness of ideas about justice. So Julius Stone rightly observed "that the theorist of justice himself may need, as we do, to make a

4. C.K. Allen, *Aspects of Justice*, 1948, p. 4.
5. See, Stone, *Human Law and Human Justice*, 1948, Meitland Sydney, p. 307.
6. C.J. Friedrich, Justice, *The Political Act, in Nomos, Justice*, 24 at 34.

conscious effort to return finally to the cardinal question: What is justice? Not only as a legal philosopher, but also as a human being, the lawyer and the jurisprudent must each try to penetrate beyond intellectual and sociological issues to face frontally the question, what, if anything, can be said about the substantive requirements or contents of the idea of justice for me and for my fellow human beings?"[7] As to the general concept of justice it is best seen as positive, ethical, and of social value. In the search for normative precepts of justice it is essential to spell out the concept of justice. For most purposes in most societies it may well be a sufficient answer to the question: "What is Justice?" to specify what kinds of conduct and procedure, in what situations, will be held "just" for that society. Certainly it may not be necessary to show that these would always and everywhere be evaluated as "just" nor even that such evaluations are more than a matter of shared subjective feelings for the time being. Yet there may also be purposes for which it does seem important to show that the offered precepts are absolute, in that they are a "universal" minimum.[8]

Thus C.J. Friedrich concludes that even if justice be seen merely in terms to accord with prevalent values three absolute criteria are inherent in it. Those are: (i) truth of the basing facts; (ii) non-arbitrariness in relating the basing facts to values, and (iii) non performance of the norms derived.[9]

At present from the interplay of man's nature and potentialities with his environment, of individuals with each

---

7. A. Brecht, *The Ultimate Standard of Justice, in Nomos Justice*, 62, referred by Stone, *Human Law and Human Justice*, 1968, p. 322.
8. Stone, *Human Law and Human Justice*, 1948, p. 324.
9. Ibid., p. 325.

other and with their cultural settings, of theories of justice with "the common sense of certain material precepts of justice which we regard as indubitable for our generation of men and in this sense quasi-absolute.[10] Stone[11] formulated some material contents of theory of justice which may not be absolute in a Kantian sense but only quasi-absolute to our present generation. These are:

(a) Social arrangement must leave everyone free to form and assert his own interests, treating every adult sane person as morally autonomous.

(b) The adjustment or shifting of advantages and burdens (including rewards and punishments) for purpose of social control through law, should proceed in terms of the goods and evils of this world only.

(c) It is always incumbent on an actor to discover with maximum possible accuracy all aspects of the situation in which he acts or fails to act.

(d) Generally all actions should respect the principle of reciprocity between persons.

(e) Generally all action should respect the principle of equality between persons.

(f) Generally any serious invasions of the socially approved distribution of advantages should be met by the grant of appropriate remedies for the persons injured.

(g) Generally contributions to socially approved arrangements shall be acknowledged, and where

---

10. Ibid., p. 341.

11. Stone formulated these contents on the basis of his discussion with his colleague A.R. Blackshield, See, *Empiricist and Rationalist Theories of Justice*, 1962, p. 481.

appropriate, shall be rewarded by protective immunities or otherwise.

(h) Generally any serious infringements of socially accepted values or invasions of the socially approved distribution of advantages shall be manifestly disapproved, where appropriate, by them out of fear of punishment.

(i) Punishment shall always respect the human dignity of the offender and shall in any case not exceed reasonable proportionality to the offence.[12]

The value and limits of pragmatic approaches to the development of justice formulated above may enable us to struggle more firmly and effectively to protect the enclaves of consensus about justice. In the words of Stone:

> Theories of justice have been seen as mediating and retrospective, affording us a degree of access to the experience of generations in winning the enclave of justice inherited. And they also challenge the present generations to approve and defend, or even to extend these enclaves and thereby to preserve the old or create new ones, from which, in turn, other theories will emerge."[13]

With this theoretical framework let us cast a look at social justice in India.

Social Justice and Constitution

The Constitution of India in the Preamble resolved to secure to all its citizens:

Justice: social, economic and political; therefore, the concept of social justice is not foreign to legal order. Social

12. Stone, op. cit., p. 341.
13. Stone, op. cit., pp. 353-54.

justice is the primary objective of the state as envisaged by our Constitution.

The Supreme Court in *Sadhuram* vs. *Pulin Behari*[14] observed that social justice is one of the aspirations of the Indian Constitution. In view of securing to all its citizens social justice our Constitution provides some Fundamental Rights in Part III some of which are available to all persons and some are enjoyable only by the citizens of India. They are:

(a) Equality before law (Article 14).

(b) Prohibition of discrimination on grounds of religion, race, caste, sex or place of birth (Article 15).

(c) Equality of opportunity in matters of public employment (Article 16).

(d) Abolition of untouchability (Article 17).

(e) Abolition of titles (Article 18).

(f) Protection of certain rights regarding freedom of speech, etc. (Article 19).

(g) Protection in respect of conviction for offences (Article 20).

(h) Protection of life and personal liberty (Article 21).

(i) Protection against arrest and detention in certain cases (Article 22).

(j) Protection of traffic in human beings and forced labour (Article 23).

(k) Prohibition of employment of children in factories or mines or in any other hazardous employment (Article 24).

(l) Freedom of religion (Articles 25-28).

---

14. *A.I.R.* 1984 SC 1471.

(m) Protection of interests of minorities (Articles 29-30).

(n) Judicial remedies for enforcement of rights conferred by this Part III of the Constitution (Article 32).

To realize the goal of social justice our Constitution also provides some directives to the state in the form of Directive Principles of State Policy (Articles 39-50) and the state shall direct its policy towards securing these objectives. The most important of these directives are:

(a) Promotion of welfare of the people (Article 38).

(b) Adequate means of livelihood; equal distribution of material resources of the community; distribution of means or production to the common good; equal pay for equal work; promotion of health and strength of workers, men, women and children; and protection against exploitation of childhood and youth (Article 39).

(c) Equal justice and free legal aid (Article 39A).

(d) Right to work, education and to public assistance in certain cases (Article 41).

(e) Just and human conditions of work and maternity relief (Article 42).

(f) Living wages for workers (Article 43).

(g) Uniform civil code (Article 44).

(h) Free and compulsory primary education for children (Article 45).

(i) Promotion of education and economic programmes (Article 46).

In interpreting the philosophy of social justice of our constitution Justice Fazal Ali observed:

> The concept of social justice is not foreign to legal justice or

> social well-being or benefit to the community rooted in the concept of justice in the 20th century. The challenge of social justice as I see it, is primarily a challenge to the society at large more than to the court immediately.Social justice is one of the aspirations of our Constitution. But we, the courts, must remember we are pledged to administer justice as by law established . . . (In) administering justice—social or legal Jurisprudonce has shifted away from finespun technicalities and abstract rules to recognition of human as human beings.[15]

The new role of the courts is rooted in a need for value-creating in situations to fill the gap left by the demise of traditional, religious, familial, and community institutions in modern society. While the legislative and administrative processes are remote the court provides an opportunity for immediate individual access to governmental decision making. The commitments to equality, liberty, fraternity and humanism reflected in the recent landmark judicial decisions are rooted in the philosophies, theologies, and moral deliberations of earlier days.[16] In order to understand fully the implications of court intervention in social issues, it is critical to look not merely at the context itself, but at the process of implementation over a period of years.[17]

The Courts and Social Justice

After our Independence a significant change has occurred in the role of judicial process in our society. Courts are now taking a leading part in the design of administration of many

15. Ibid., para 70.
16. Michael A. Rabell, "Judicial Activism and the Courts 'New Role," *Journal of Social Policy* (USA) Sprıng, 1982, vol. 12, no. 4.
17. David J. Rathman, "The Courts and Social Reform" *Law and Human Behavior*, 1982, vol. 6, no. 2.

state services — including services for the mentally ill and retarded, for prison populations, for public welfare recipients, and for abused children and other dependent persons. With that end in view the Supreme Court of India evolved a new mechanism of public interest litigation or social interest litigation in the early 1980s. In the 1950s and 1960s the role of judiciary more or less remained a sober manifestation of the movement for social justice based on progressive values. While other institutions have progressively shone, the judiciary remains a uniquely situated instrument for social justice, perhaps the only effective force for challenging the institutions of the welfare state. Echoing Richard of America I may say:

> This image of the judiciary allows progressive values to survive in an age that generally mistrusts institutions. It is central to this view that courts alone stand above the battle of bureaucratic forces. . . Long nurtured ideals are not given up easily, however. And in the past several years, the image of courts as both bureaucratically pure and ideologically progressive has been reinforced by some extravagant philosophical arguments including the claim that judges are the only social authorities able to define social values on the level of objective truth.[18]

Judicial activism figures prominently in contemporary India with the active assistance of social activists and public interest litigators for vindication of governmental commitment to welfare and social justice. One of the meanings of judicial activism is that the function of the courts is not merely to interpret the law but to make it imaginatively share the passion of the Constitution for social justice.[19] Thus, we have the "*goal-*

---

18. Richard Gaskins, "Second Thoughts on Law as an Instrument of Social Change," *Law and Human Behavior*, 1982, vol. 6, no. 2.

19. V.R. Krishna Iyer, *Democracy of Judicial Remedies, a Rejoinder to Hidayatullah*, 4th Sec. 1984, pp. 43-54.

oriented" approach of Chief Justice P.N. Bhagwati, *"humanist-reformist"* approach of Justice Krishna Iyer and *"community-oriented"* approach of Justice Ranganath Misra. This judicial activism has produced many enclaves of creativity, e.g. human rights jurisprudence, bonded labour jurisprudence, and many others. Social justice in India is a Constitutional guarantee so as to bring the "rule of law" closer to the "rule of life."[20] Justice according to the law is that justice which people holding power of the state may consider it necessary or justified to provide. The expectation is that when power defines justice it will enforce its definition. If this does not happen, legal justice itself may furnish a standard to question the legitimacy of power. In the law, then, we may expect at the very best, not the power of justice but justice of power.[21]

In the recent years the judicial role in public policy has greatly expanded and the present generation has witnessed a remarkable expansion of judicial participation in the implementation of public policy. Plaintiffs increasingly have asked courts not simply to correct isolated and discrete violations of law but also to effect systemic reform of entire institutions or programmes. Court has become the principal forum for the pursuit of structural reform by many groups most disaffected with the delivery of governmental services. In responding to these demands, judges have found themselves in the unfamiliar position of designing and superintending major changes in institutions. Judges have not sought merely

20. Parmanand Singh, "Judicial Socialism and Problems of Liberation : Myth and Truth," *Journal of the Indian Law Institute*, vol. 28, No. 3, (July-September 1986), p. 337.

21. Upendra Baxi, "Judicial Discourse : Dialectics of the Face and The Mask," *Journal the Indian Law Institute*, vol. 35, No. 1 and 2, p. 1.

to monitor the activities of these institutions but have attempted to restructure them, to change their process and policies.

This judicial activism, sharing the passion of our Constitution for social justice started with the Maneka Gandhi Case[22] whereby fundamental right of personal liberty has been converted into a regime of positive human rights unknown in previous Constitutional diction. Thereafter, gradually the Supreme Court, particularly some Rights and Directive Principles of State Policy and thus we got an explosion of rights. In this way the courts try to force the government to realize the new concept of social justice in the cases of *Sunil Batra* vs. *Delhi Administration*[23] (right against bondage); *People's Union for Democratic Rights* vs. *Union of India*,[24] *Olga Tellis* vs. *Bombay Municipal Corporation*)[25] (right to livelihood); *R.E.E. Kendra Dehradun* vs. *State of Uttar Pradesh*[26] (rights against environmental pollution), (or *M.C. Metha* vs. *Union of India*);[27] *Upendra Baxi* vs. *State of Uttar Pradesh*[28] (right to human dignity); *Sheela Barse* vs. *Union of India*;[29] (right to legal aid); *M.K. Sharma* vs. *Bharat Electronics Ltd.*[30] (right to have safety and protection to the workers); or *Sankar* vs. *Durgapur Projects Limited.*[31] Relying on *Olga Tellis* the court held that compelling a person to live in

22. 1978 (2) SCR 621.
23. *A.I.R.* 1980 SC. 1974.
24. 1984 (3) S.C.C. 161.
25. 1982 (2) S.C.C. 235.
26. 1935 (3) S.C.C. 545.
27. *A.I.R.* 1985 SC. 652.
28. 1986 (2) S.C.C. 176.
29. 1986 (4) S.C.C. 106.
30. 1986 (3) S.C.C. 632.
31. 1987 (3) S.C.C. 231.

sub-human conditions amounts to taking away of his life. *Poola Bhaskara Vijay Kumar* vs. *State of Andhra Pradesh*[32] [right of prisoner to get wages (Article 21)]; *People's Union of Democratic Rights* vs. *Police Commissioner, Delhi Police*[33] (against police brutality); *Krishen Pattanayak* vs. *State of Orissa*[34] (victims of starvation death in the district of Kalahandi, Orissa); *Vistha Leet* vs. *Union of India*[35] (child abuse and forced prostitution) Article 39(e) and (f), Article 23 child abuse and traffic in human beings (Immoral Traffic Prevention Act 1956). In *M.C. Mehta* vs. *Union of India*[36] the court agreed that law alone could not help in restoring a balance in the bi-sphere disturbance due to pollution. In *Delhi Judicial Service Association, Tis Hazari Courts, Delhi* vs. *State of Gujarat*[37] (also known as Nadiad case) (police brutality against GJM Nadiad) and in *Banwari Sewa Ashram* vs. *U.P.*[38] where *adivasis* and other backward class people used forest as their habitat and means of livelihood, and parts of such forests were declared as reserved. In these cases the judges maintain that in a developing society judicial activism is essential for participative justice and the bureaucrats as well as the elected reprevenïatives will have to face the judicial admonition and pay the penalty if the people in misery cry for justice.[39] But in *State of Himachal Pradesh* vs. *Umedram*[40] the Supreme Court considered the question whether the right to

32. *A.I.R.* 1988 Cal 137.
33. *A.I.R.* 1988 A.P. 295.
34. 1989 (4) S.C.C. 730.
35. *A.I.R.* 1989 SC 677.
36. 1990 (3) S.C.C. 318.
37. 1991 (2) S.C.C. 353.
38. 1991 (4) S.C.C. 406.
39. *A.I.R.* 1992 SC. 920.
40. Paramannand Singh, op. cit., p. 339.

life includes the right to have usable road for the residents of hilly areas. Answering the question in the affirmative the court speaking through S. Mukharjee J. observed:

> Every person is entitled to life as enjoined in Article 21 and in the facts of this case read in conjunction with Article 19(1) (d) . . . and in the background of Article 38(2) . . . every person has a right under Article 19(1) (d) to move freely throughout the territory of India and he has also a right under Article 21 to his life and that right under Article 21 embraces not only physical existence of life but for residents of hilly areas access to road is access to life itself.[41]

The court cited the cases in respect of *Santram*[42] *Kharak Singh* vs. *Union of India*[43] *A.V. Nachane* vs. *Union of India*[44] *Olga Tellis,*[45] *Municipal Council, Ratlam* vs. *Vardhichand*[46] and *Francis Coralie Mullin* vs. *Administrator, Union Territory of Delhi.*[47] Stretching the meaning of right to life and linking it to other fundamental rights the Supreme Court has opened a Pandora's box. Chhatrapati Singh has aptly put the doctrinal puzzles thus:

Once it is agreed that the right to life includes the right to having roads in accordance with Article 19(1)(d) . . . one may as well claim that it entails the right to having a house in accordance with Article 19(1)(e) for one cannot reside without a house.

Prof. Upendra Baxi commenting upon judicial activism through public interest litigation which he called Social Actions Litigation (SAL) observed:

---

41. 1986 (2) S.C.C. 68.
42. Ibid., pp. 74-75.
43. *A.I.R.* 1960 SC. 932.
44. *A.I.R.* 1963 SC. 1295.
45. 1982 (1) S.C.C. 205
46. 1982 (3) S.C.C. 545.
47. 1980 (4) S.C.C. 162.

> The judicial discourse in SAL seeks to return to the simple idea that wherever there is power there is accountability, on the assumption that wherever there is accountability power would know its limits and proper uses . . . but as things are, judicial intervention for justice has, at least, taken the momentous step of ushering in accountability in the limited sense. This is not a small gain.[48]

The ambiguity and uncertainty over meaning of right to life led Justice P.B. Sawant to state the following:

> The country has so far not found it feasible to incorporate the right to livelihood as a fundamental right in the Constitution. This is because the country has so far not attained the capacity to guarantee it and not because it considers it any fundamental to life. Advisedly, therefore, it has been placed in the chapter on Directive Principles, Article 41 of which enjoins upon the state to make effective provision for securing the same within the limits of its economic capacity and development.[49]

The emergence of PIL and SAL had made a good beginning but this issue has been quickly oversubscribed. Thus, it has resulted in dislocation of the judicial schedule of the Apex Court. It has also created a tug of war between the judiciary and the two other limbs of the state — the Legislature and the executive. Most of the decisions of the Supreme Court in the newly-fashioned segments of its jurisdiction have been ignored by the executive. Thus, the over-activism of the court in PIL or SAL cases has reduced the effectiveness of its rulings.[50] The cases of Sebastian *Hongray* vs. *Union of India*.[51]

48. 1981 (1) S.C.C. 608.

49. Baxi, op. cit., 12.

50. *Delhi Development Horticulture Employees Union* vs. *Delhi Administration A.I.R.* 1992 SC 789 at 795.

51. K.C. Joshi, "Judicial Process : Recent Trends," *The Journal of Indian Law Institute*, vol. 34, No. 1, 1992.

Upendra Baxi vs. *State of U.P.*, *Bhim Singh* vs. *Delhi Petroleum Gas Leakage* Case[52] and *Sheela Barse* vs. *Union of India*[53] are some of the instances of such defiance by the executive.

The expansion of judicial role in public policy often required the court to order massive increases in expenditures, wholesale administrative reorganization and complete revision of operational practices. Sometimes the courts have exercised legislative functions by setting policy standards for the operation of state and central government programmes, including the setting of budgetary requirements. This enlargement of judicial function is a qualitative change that has emerged in our legal system in the recent years.

That is why Bodenheimer observed:

> There may be situations where stagnation of delay can be overcome only by a judicial decision-maker who being convinced that the preponderant values of the community are wholly obsolete or unreasonable is willing to take risk and is determined to chart a new course into the future. Progress often depends on the courageous, decisive and anti-traditional action of great men.[54]

Therefore, Lord Denning has rightly observed:

> If the truth is recognized then we may hope to escape from the dead hand of the past and consciously mould new principles to meet the need of the present.[55]

So judicial activism is desirable, but within defined limits. In a democracy the judiciary cannot supervise the legislative mandate or executive authority. W. Friedman observes:

---

52. *A.I.R.* 1984 SC. 1026.
53. 1984 (4) S.C.C. 106.
54. 1984 (4) S.C.C. 677.
55. *A.I.R.* 1987 SC. 1086.

> In modern democratic society the judge must steer his way between the Scylla of subservience to government and the charybdis of remoteness from constantly changing social pressures and economic needs.[56]

Social and political reforms can hardly be introduced through judicial process. Judicial process must function within the prevailing social, economic and political atmospheres.[57] Judicial process can only give direction to the spirit of law. Basic reforms whether social or political do not fall within the jurisdiction of the courts.[58] In spite of this the modern jurisprudence no longer revolves round the question "whether judges find or invent law." And the courts emerge as "the capital of law's empire and the judges as their princes."[59]

Social Justice and Indian Judicial System

A discussion on the need for a viable judicial system may start with the following luminous observations of Justice Eichelbaum of the High Court of New Zealand:

> Any democracy worth its name must provide adequate means of dispute resolution. And while we have all become accustomed to think of the Westminster model as the ideal form of machinery, Lord Devlin said in *'The Judge, the Judge,'* the obligation of the state is to provide as many modes of trial as are necessary to cover the variety of disputes that may have commonly arisen, so that for each type there is an available process that will offer a reasonable standard of justice at reasonable cost.[60]

---

56. *A.I.R.* 1988 SC 2211.
57. Bodenheimer, *Jurisprudence*, 1987, p. 443.
58. See, N.K. Chakrabarti, *Principles of Legislations and Legislative Drafting*, 1994, p. 175.
59. W. Friedmann, *Law in a Changing Society*, 1972, p. 88.
60. Lord Denning, "Judges and the Judicial power" in Rajeev Dhavan ed., *Judges and the Judicial Power*, 1985, pp. 1-4.

But the judicial system introduced by the British in India is still continuing with its inherent problem of arrears. From Civil Justice Committee 1924 to the Arrears Committee 1989-90 through Arrears Committee 1949, 1967, the survey was conducted by the Government of India, Arrears Committee 1972 and Law Commission Reports 79th, 80th, 121st, and 124th, which clearly revealed that our judicial system was contributing to the mounting arrears of cases.[61] The Law Commission of India in its 124th *Report on the High Court Arrears — A Fresh Look* observed:

> Unless, therefore, the jurisdiction of the High Courts is substantially curtailed, simultaneously providing effective forum for judicial review enjoyed by the High Courts, the situation by cosmetic peripheral changes is not likely to improve and the situation which was considered "alarming" can now be described as catastrophic, crisis-ridden, almost unmanageable imposing such an immeasurable burden on the system which led the former Chief Justice of India warning that the system is about to crash.[62]

To overcome this alarming situation the Arrears Committee 1989-90 constituted by the Government of India on the recommendation of the conference of Chief Justices with Justice V.S. Malimath as Chairman and Justice P.D. Desai and Justice A.S. Anand as members, recommended alternative modes and forums for dispute resolution such as setting up of Administrative Tribunals, Tribunals, Educational Tribunals, National and State level Industrial Relations Commissions, Conciliation Courts on the model of the scheme evolved by the Himachal Pradesh High Court, but no effort has been made

61. K.C. Joshi, "Judicial Procees : Recent Trends" in *Journal of ILI*, vol. 34, January-March, 1992, p. 10.
62. R. Dowrkin, *The Law's Empire* 225, 1986, quoted by Upendra Baxi, in 12 *Delhi Law Review*, 13, 1990.

either to amend the Civil or Criminal Procedure Code to streamline our judicial system for dealing with the huge volume of arrears, on account of fast population increase so as to promote "Justice — social, political and economic." The executive as well as the legislative organs of our state failed to show discernible concern and to evolve a viable legal system which is a *sine qua non* for achieving justice. The timely filling up of vacancies of posts of judges in the High Courts and in the subordinate courts still remained a crying need of the judiciary which started with Justice Ranking in 1924 and ended with Justice Malimath in 1990 through four Arrears Committees and Sixth Law Commission Reports. The solution to the problem lies in characterizing the judicial role as one which has moved in the direction of separating questions of value from question of instrumentalism. We may look at history to observe how political and judicial institutions have responded in the past to similar pressures; the emergence of equity jurisdiction, and the move towards administrative regulation in the twentieth century. There has been a tendency to characterize judges as instrumentalists and the courts as one member of a team of instrumentalists to achieve social justice as enshrined in the Preamble of our Constitution.

Therefore there is now a strong need in India to have co-ordination between the executive and judicial organs of the state. In fact, there is no such legislation in India. What is happening in case of most of the social reform legislations in India is that whenever there appears "heat" regarding any matter in the society, the Legislature passes a law on it. But after the passing of the law, for want of implementation, people, especially the masses, never receive "light" from that heat.[63] So we need to develop a viable judicial system by

63. See, 61 (9), 1987, Australia, I.J., p. 456.

changing our existing procedural laws and taking necessary steps for timely filing up of the vacancies of the posts of judges in all courts. But law alone or the courts alone cannot bring social justice. The law enforcement agency, i.e. the executive has an important role in the programme of social justice. The development of delivery system of justice is a part and parcel of the programme of social justice which depends very much upon an integral approach and correlation among the three organs of the states because "to walk alone is to work in vain."[64]

From the foregoing analysis it may be inferred that heroics of some activist judges cannot bring social justice through PIL or SAL only. The implementation of this progressive values attitude requires return to instrumental thinking and revitalization of institutions and programmes of social justice. This task cannot be placed within the exclusive domain of the courts. Progressive judges can no doubt develop basic values in society. Unless the spirit of the age inclines towards progressive values, sooner or later these values will be discarded by even the judiciary and this is discernible in the beginning of the 1990s in the Supreme Court of India. The judiciary can supply powerful impetus to broader policies for social justice as the relationship of courts with other institutions is a partnership combining instrumental rationality. The twenty-first century will perhaps answer the question whether our society is ready to reject its present anti-institutional stance and put new confidence in institutions for social justice other than the courts.

---

64. See, *Report of the Arrears Committee*, 1989-90 published by the Supreme Court of India, 1990, pp. 50-53.

Epilogue

Now in this chapter a total recall of previous chapters can be undertaken and final conclusions can be systematically presented. To arrive at a sharp focus Dr Ambedkar was a genius scholar who was not only an economist but a philosopher of original thinking as well. In this work the socio-legal philosophy of Ambedkar was unfolded systematically and his original reflections have been presented. This is the first work of its kind which can be described as unique because it echoes a true socio-legal philosophy which Ambedkar had evolved on the basis of his grass-roots thinking. This work is based on Constituent Assembly Debates as well as original articles, speeches and writings of Ambedkar on Indian Constitution, as well as on the social and legal system.

In the first part of this chapter a summary of previous chapters can be briefly presented.

In the first chapter, background regarding social philosophy of Dr Ambedkar has been properly analyzed. It is very interesting to observe that, Ambedkar derives the concept of equality and social justice on the basis of Buddhist philosophy. He had thoroughly understood the progressive tenets of Buddhism as a religious philosophy. He often brings to notice that he has derived the concepts like liberty, equality, fraternity and social justice not from French Revolution, but from the all-comprehensive philosophy of Lord Buddha. In this chapter the origin of caste attitudes towards weaker sections is discussed. Untouchability has been described here as leprosy of Hinduism and various approaches for its removal have also been discussed. Further it has been noted how Ambedkar perceived the removal of untouchability through adoption of constitutional measures.

The second chapter, crystallizes the economic philosophy of Ambedkar based on his original works. In this chapter Ambedkar's three major economic studies such as Provincial finances in British India during East India Company's rule, his perception regarding the problem of Rupee, and his understanding of agricultural problems in India with special reference to landless labourers, were studied one after another. The theme of this work pinpoints that, if we carefully study Ambedkar's economic works we can solve chronic economic problems which are making India to suffer. Finally his ideas have also been discussed in the new situation with special reference to globalization.

The third chapter is the backbone of the study, which discusses the contribution of Ambedkar to social philosophy. This chapter has brought to light three basic areas of social justice: First, regarding emancipation of untouchables and their empowerment; Secondly, regarding women's emancipation and Ambedkar's ideas to strengthen Indian women in a relevant manner. This work of Ambedkar really presents him on the top of the social philanthrophists because he brought the philosophy of Mahatma Phule in action by freeing Indian women from the clutches of Manu through his legal reforms. His ideas about welfare of minorities have also been discussed in this chapter.

The fourth chapter, debates on Mandal Commission and judicial decisions. In this chapter Ambedkar's progressive ideas about welfare of other backward classes (OBCs) have been discussed and how these ideas are reflected in the Mandal Commission's recommendations have been carefully interpreted. This chapter shows the progressive forward-looking approach of Ambedkar.

The fifth chapter deals with rights and values which are very significant in the protection of Indian democracy. Ambedkar was a champion of democratic values throughout his debates on Indian Constitution. A special case study about Article 356 has been presented in this chapter, which is a core contribution of this work.

The sixth chapter is based on a basic understanding of Ambedkar's ideas about welfare of weaker sections. According to Ambedkar political democracy cannot be successful unless and until it is transformed into social and economic democracy. A nation can be strong and able if the weaker sections are transformed into healthy social groups based on principles of equality. In this chapter the different views of Ambedkar on the empowerment of weaker sections have been presented.

The seventh chapter is a basic understanding of Ambedkar's legal philosophy. His views on court justice and social justice in India have been discussed and correlated here. Here, his concept of justice based on his theories has been very well presented. Further he has suggested normative component about social action which is very much useful for bringing modern India on the path of progress. The social justice in Indian judicial system perceived by Ambedkar has been presented in a nutshell.

As background to these chapters now a philosophical review about this work can be presented below. This part thus presents a new theoretical frame work.

Ambedkar considered the caste system in Hindu society as a great enemy of social harmony in this country. He could not succeed in abolishing the caste system among the Hindus and, therefore, in disgust renounced Hinduism and embraced Buddhism on October 14, 1956. In my opinion, it is a matter of shame for the Hindu society that it could not retain such a great scholar and a nationalist to the core in its fold because of the rigid practice of caste system, particularly in villages. The day will come when we get freedom from the stranglehold of the rigid caste system. Ambedkar's lifelong sacrifices for this cause will not go in vain and will, we hope and pray, eventually bear fruit.

Thus, to take an overview this work finally presents the socio-legal philosophy of Ambedkar in a new angle. Ambedkar is mostly relevant for building modern India on the basis of progressive values. The constitutional culture which is based on liberty, equality, fraternity and social justice is truly a contribution of Ambedkar's genius thinking. His philosophy can provide a new light for India marching ahead towards becoming a super power in CE 2020. First there is birth of philosophy and then there comes action. Ambedkar has provided both socio-legal philosophy and programme of action. If India can march ahead, on this programme of action, India can be a stronger, more united and more integrated nation in the twenty-first century.

Appendix – I

Life and Mission of Dr Babasaheb Ambedkar (1891-1956)

14th April, 1891 : Dr Bhimrao Ramji Ambedkar allas Babasaheb was born at Mahu (Mhow) in the then Central Province (Present State of Madhya Pradesh).

1897-1907 : Bhimrao attended primary schol at Dapoll and Satara. He completed his high school education at Satara and Bombay. He passed his Matriculation Examination in 1907 from the Elphinstone High School, Bombay.

April 1908 . Bhimrao married to Ramabai.

1912 : Bhimrao Ambedkar passed his B.A. Examination with English and Persian language as the special subjects from Elphinstone College, Bombay.

2 Feb. 1913 : Bhimrao's father, Subhedar Ramji died.

4 June 1913 : Bhimrao Ambedkar was selected by the Maharaja of Baroda State, Sayajirao Gaikwad for going to the USA to attain higher education. Bhimrao Ambedkar arrived in New York in the third week of July 1913 and joined the Columbia University.

1915 : Ambedkar obtained his M.A. degree for this thesis "Ancient Indian Commerce".

May 1916 : Ambedkar read a paper on "Castes in India, Their Mechanism, Genesis and Development" before the Anthropology Seminar of Dr Golden Weiser.

June 1916 : Ambedkar's another thesis "National Dividend of India

— A Historical and Analytical Study" was accepted by the Columbia University in the second week of June, 1916. Eight Years after this Messrs P.S. King and Son Ltd., London, published an extension of the thesis entitled, "The Evolution of Provincial Finance in Brtitish India". The Columbia University awarded the degree of Ph. D. to Ambedkar for the thesis.

Oct. 1916 : Ambedkar was admitted in Oct. 1916 to the London School of Economics and Political Science for the study of Economics.

Sept. 1917 : Ambedkar went to Baroda in accordance with a bond signed by him to serve the State of Baroda.

Nov. 1918 : Ambedkar accepted the post of professor of Political Economy in the Sydenham College, Bombay.

1919 : Ambedkar was called upon to give evidence before the Southborough Committee.

31 Jan. 1920 : Ambedkar started a fortnightly paper "Mook Nayak" (Leader of the Dumb), with financial help from Chhatrapati Shahu, the Maharaja of Kolhapur.

21 March 1920 : Ambedkar presided over a Conference of the Untouchables at Mangaon in the Kolhapur State. Chhatrapati Shahu of Kolhapur attended it.

May 1920 : Ambedkar attended First All India Conference in the last week of May 1920 at Nagpur convened by untouchables and presided over by Shahu Maharaja of Kolhapur.

June 1921 : Ambedkar submitted his thesis titled "Provincial Decentralization of Imperial Finance in British India" for which he was awarded the degree of M.Sc.

Oct. 1922 : Ambedkar completed his thesis "The Problem of the Rupee" and submitted to the University of London for which he was awarded the degree of D.Sc. in 1923. He was also called to the Bar.

April 1923 : Ambedkar returned to India with degrees of Barrister at-Law and D.Sc. from London University. He had also completed his advanced studies at the Bonn University in Germany.

4 Aug. 1993 :Mr S.K. Bole Resolution was adopted by the Bombay Legislative Council, which allowed the Untouchables to use all public watering places, wells and dharamashalas.

20 July 1924 : "The Bahishkrit Hitakarini Sabha" was founded at a meeting held at the Damodar Hall, Bombay.

January 1927 : Ambedkar was nominated to the Bombay Legislative Council by the Governor of Bombay.

1927 : The Mahad Municipality had thrown open its tank called the Chowdar Tank in 1926 to the Untouchables in pursuance of the Bole resolution of 1923, but the untoachables could not exercise their right due to the hostility of the caste Hindus.

20 March, 1927 : A Conference by the Kolaba Dist. Depressed Classes at Mahad. Speech by Ambedkar.

March 1927 :Peaceful March of the delegates to the Chowdar Tank, to assert their right of taking water from the tank. Attack on the delegates of the conference by the caste Hindus at Mahad.

3 April 1927 : "Bahishkrit Bharat" a fortnightly Marathi Paper started by Ambedkar in Bombay.

4 Aug. 1927 :The Mahad Municipality revoked its resolution of 1924 under which it had declared the Chowdar Tank open to the Depressed classes.

15 Sept. 1927 : Ambedkar decided to launch a struggle for establishing the right of the Depressed classes to use the water of the Tank at Mahad and announced Dec. 25 and 26, 1927 as the dates for offering the second satyagraha.

Dec. 25, 1927 : Second Conference at Mahad held, Resolution was ado[pted by which he declaration of human right was passed. The satyagraha was postponed.

19 March, 1928 : A bill was introduced in the Legistative Council for the abolition of the Mahar Waten.

June 1928 : Ambedkar accepted an appointment as an acting Professor at the Govt. Law College, Bombay.

Aug. 1928 : Ambedkar submitted a memorandum to the Simon Commission on behalf of the Bahishkrit Hitkarni Sabha, demanding Joint electorates with reservation of seats for the Depressed Classes.

3 March 1930 : The Nasik, Kalaram Temple entrance Satyagraha commenced under his leadership and the gates of the temple were closed and barricated. The agitation continued up to the end of October 1935.

Nov. 17-21, 1930 : Ambedkar made very impressive speeches at the Round Table conference. He Submitted to the Minorities Sub–Committee a scheme of Political Safeguards for Protection of the Depressed Classes in the future constitution of a self-governing India.

Aug. 14, 1931 : Ambedkar-Gandhi meeting Manibhuvan, Malabar Hill in Bombay.

Aug. 20, 1932 : The British Prime Minister declared his Award on the communal issue in India under which the Depressed Classes were granted separate seats in the Provincial Assemblies and the righ of double vote.

1932 : Gandhiji declared from Yervada jail his resolve to fast unto death if the separate electorates granted to the Depressed Classes were not abolished.

24 Sept. 1932 : The Poona Pact was signed by Ambedkar.

May 27, 1935 : Death of Mrs. Ramabai Ambedkar, wife of Ambedkar which was a shocking event to him.

June 1, 1935 : Ambedkar acepted the appointment as Principal of Govt. Law College, Mombay.

13 Oct. 1935 : Ambedkar announced at the Conference at Yeola his intention of leaving the fold of Hinduism and embrace some other religion.

1935 : The undelivered speech to the Jat-Pat Todak Mandal at Lahore at its Annual Conference, was published by Ambedkar under the title "Annihilation of Castes".

May 30, 31, 1936 : The Mahar Conference of the Depressed Classes met at Dadar under the presidentship of Shri B.S. Venkatrao, a Depressed Class leader from Hyderabad in Andhra pradesh. Ambedkar addressed it. The conference declared by a resolution that they were prepared to change their religion *en masse*.

Aug. 1936 : Ambedkar founded a new political party called the "Independent Labour Party".

Mrch 18, 1937 : The protracted Mahad Chowdar Tank water case was decided in favour of the Depressed Classes by the Bombay High Court.

Dec. 1940 : Ambedkar's book, *Thoughts on Pakistan*, was published.

July 18, 1942 : All India Scheduled Castes Federation was formed at Nagpur.

July 20, 1942 : Ambedkar accepted his appointment as Member in the Viceroy's Executive Council to look after the Labour portfolio.

Jan. 19, 1943 : Ambedkar delivered a speech on the occasion of the birth anniversary of Justice M.G. Ranade, at Poona. This speech is published in a book form entitled. "Ranade, Gandhi and Jinnah".

June 1945 : Ambedkar's book entitled "What Congress and Gandhi have done to the Untouchables" was published.

June 20, 1945 : Ambedkar founded the People's Education Society at Bombay. The Siddarth College was started at Bombay.

Oct. 1945-46 : Ambedkar's book "Who were The Shudras" was published. Ambedkar was elected to the Constituent Assembly from Bengal.

March 1947 : Ambedkar's brochure "States and Minorities" published.

Aug. 3, 1947 : Ambedkar was sworn in as the First Law Minister in the Ministry of Pt. Jawaharlal Nehru.

Aug. 29, 1947 : Ambedkar was appointed as Chairman of the Drafting Committee to write the Constitution of India.

Feb. 1948 : Ambedkar completed the Draft Constitution and submitted it to the President of the Constituent Assembly.

April 15, 1948 : Ambedkar married Dr Miss Sharda Kabir, a Saraswat Brahmin at New Delhi.

Nov. 4, 1948 : Ambedkar introduced the Draft Constitution in the Constiuent Assembly.

Nov. 25, 1949 : Ambedkar, the architect of the Constitution delivered his most important speech to reply to the debate on the third reading of the Constitution.

Nov. 26, 1949 : The Constitution was adopted by the Constituent Assembly.

Sept. 1, 1950 : The foundation stone of the new building for the Milind Maha Vidyalaya at Aurangabd was laid by Dr Rajendra Prasad, the President of the Indian Republic.

May 1950 : Ambedkar visited Ceylon and participated in Word Buddhist Conference.

Feb. 5, 1951 : Ambedkar introduced the Hindu Code Bill in the Parliament.

Sep. 27, 1951 : Ambedkar resigned his seat from the Nehru Ministry. He was elected to the Rajya Sabha from the Bombay State.

5 June, 1952 : Dr Ambedkar was awarded the honorary degree of Doctor of Laws (LL.D) by the Columbia University in New York.

12 Jan. 1953 : The Osmania University, Hyderabad conferred the degree of D. Lit. (Doctor of Literature) on Ambedkar.

3 Oct. 1954 : Ambedkar delivered a talk in the series "My personal Philosophy" on All India Radio.

1st Week Dec. 1954 : Ambedkar participated in the Third International Buddhist Conference at Rangoon, Burma.

May 1955 : Ambedkar founded the "Buddbhist Society of India" at Bombay. In the same year he started "*Prabuddha Bharat*", a weekly.

May 1956 : Ambedkar delivered a talk on the BBC on the subject "Why I like Buddhism and how it is useful to the world?"

May 1956 : Ambedkar delivered a talk on the Voice of America on the "Future of Democracy in India".

June 1956 : Founded Sidharth College of Law at Bombay.

14 Oct. 1956 : Vijaya Dashmi Day : Dr Babasaheb Ambedkar and Maisabeb Mrs. Savitabai Ambedkar embraced Buddhism at the hands of Mahasthavir Chandramani at Diksha Bhoomi, Nagpur.

15 Oct. 1956 : Ambedkar initiated (Dikshya) lakhs of his followers into Buddhism.

Nov. 1956 : Ambedkar participated in the World Buddhist Conference at Kathmandu, Nepal where he delivered his speech "Buddha and Karl Marx".

6 Dec. 1956 : Mahaparinirvan of Babasaheb Ambedkar at his residence at Alipur Road in New Delhi.

7 Dec. 1956 : The earthly remains of Ambedkar were cremated at the Dadar Choupati, the present Chaityabhumi with full honours in the presence of lakhs of his sorrow-striken followers.

Appendix – II

Books Written by Bharat Ratna Dr B.R. Ambedkar

1.	Castes in India	1916
2.	The National Dividend of India	1916
3.	Small Holdings In India	1917
4.	The Problem of Rupee	1923
5.	Evolution Of Provincial Finance In British India	1925
6.	Annihilation Of Caste	1936
7.	Federation versus Freedom	1939
8.	Thoughts On Pakistan	1940
9.	Mr Gandhi and Emancipation Of Untouchables	1943
10.	Ranade, Gandhi and Jinnah	1943
11.	Communal Deadlock and how to Solve it.	1945
12.	What Congress and Gandhi have done to untouchables?	1946
13.	Who were the Sudras?	1946
14.	States and Minorities	1946

15. The History Of Indian Currency and Banking 1947
16. The Untouchables, Who were they? 1948
17. Maharashtra as a Linguistic Province 1948
18. The Rise and Fall Of Hindu Women 1951
19. Thoughts On Linguistic States 1955
20. Buddha and His Dhamma 1956

The unpublished written Books, Articles, other material and literary work written by Ambedkar had been published by the Government of Maharashtra under the title:

DR BABASAHEB AMBEDKAR
WRITINGS AND SPEECHES

The detailed list is given as under:

Vol. 1: Castes in India and 11 other essays. Pages 520, Rs. 40

Vol. 2: Dr Ambedkar In the Bombay Legislature, with the Simon Commission and at the Round Table Conference 1927 to 1939. *Pages 823, Rs. 80*

Vol. 3: Philosophy of Hinduism. India and the Pre-requisites of Communism. Revolution and Counter-Revolution. Buddha or Karl Marx. *Pages 508, Rs. 40*

Vol. 4: Riddles in Hinduism. *Pages 368, Rs. 35*

Vol. 5: Essay on Untouchable and Un-touchability.

Vol. 6: The Evolution of Provincial Finance in British-India. The Problem of the Rupee. *Pages 712, Rs. 55*

Vol. 7: Who were the Shudras? The Untouchables. *Pages 390, Rs. 40*

Vol. 8: Pakistan or the Partition of India. *Pages 510, Rs. 40*

Vol. 9: What Congress and Gandhi have done to the Untouchables. Mr Gandhi and the Emancipation of the Untouchables. *Pages 500, Rs. 50*

Vol. 10: Dr Ambedkar as Member of the Governor-General's Executive Council 1942-46. *Pages 1080, Rs. 95*

Vol. 11: The Buddha and His Dhamma. *Pages 620, Rs. 70*

Vol. 12: Unpublished Writings. Ancient Indian Commerce, Notes on Laws. Writing for a visa. Miscellaneous notes etc. *Pages 794, Rs. 95*

Vol. 13: Dr Ambedkar as the Principal Architect of the Constitution of India. *Pages 1240, Rs. 190*

Vol. 14: **in two parts** Dr Ambedkar and Hindu Code Bill. *Parges 1385, Rs. 110 (Overseas $ 10)*

Vol. 15: Dr Ambedkar as Free India's First Law Minister and Member of Opposition in Indian Parliament (1947 to 1956). *Pages 1110, Rs. 110 (overseas $ 10)*

Vol. 16: Dr Ambedkar's (i) The Pali Grammar (ii) The Pali Dictionary (a) Pali into English, (b) Pali into English, Marathi, Hindi and Gujarathi. (iii) Bouddha Pooja Path. *Pages 752, Rs. (overseas $ 10)*

Vol. 17: Dr Babasaheb Ambedkar and his Egalitarian Revolution (parts 1 to 3) part 2, *Pages 546, Rs. 125 (overseas $ 25)*

Vol. 18: Dr Babasaheb Ambedkar's Speeches. *Pages 1878 Rs. 300*

Other Published Volumes

Source material on Dr Babasaheb Ambedkar and the Movement of the Untouchables.

Vol. 1: Pages 468, Rs. 1000 (out of print)

Vol. 2: (Marathi)

Dr Babasaheb Ambedkar. Pages 500, Rs. 75.

Forthcoming Volumes

Vol. 19: Dr Babasaheb Ambedkar

Vol. 20: Dr Ambedkar's Correspondence

Vol. 21: Dr Ambedkar in Photographs

Bibliography

Allen, C.K., *Aspects of Justice,* 1948.

Ambedkar, B.R., *Anihilation of Caste.*

Ambedkar, B.R., *Case for Hindu Code,* 1949.

Ambedkar, B.R., *Constituent Assembly Debates,* all vols.

Ambedkar, B.R., *The Report of the Backward Classes Commission,* vol. 3, 1956.

Ambedkar, B.R., *The Rise and Fall of the Hindu Woman,* 1965.

Ambedkar, B.R., *Writings and Speeches,* vol. 2.

Ambedkar, B.R, *Writings and Speeches,* Government of Maharashtra, vol. 6, 1989.

Bakshi, P.M., "Reservation for Backward Classes — Some Reflections", in the *Journal of Indian Law Institute,* vol. 2, April-June, 1985, no. 2.

Baxi, Upendra, "Judicial Discourse: Dialectics of the Face and The Mask," *Journal the Indian Law Institute,* vol. 35, no. 1 and 2.

Bodenheimer, *Jurisprudence,* 1987.

Brecht, A., *The Ultimate Standard of Justice, in Nomos Justice,* 62, referred by Stone, *Human Law and Human Justice,* 1968.

Budget of 2001-02, Government of India.

Chakrabarti, N.K., *Principles of Legislations and Legislative Drafting,* 1994.

Chalam, K.S. and G. Nancharaiah (ed.), *Relevance of Ambedkarism in India,* Ambedkar University, Lucknow, Ambedkar on Economic Development.

Chapman, J., *Justice and Fairness.*

Choudhary, S.N., "Ambedkar, Caste and Hindu Religion: An Analysis", S.S. Shashi ed. *Ambedkar and Social Justice* in New Delhi: Publication Division, Government of India, 1992, vol. I.

Das, Bhagwan, *Relevance of Ambedkar.*

Denning (Lord), "Judges and the Judicial power" in Rajeev Dhavan ed., *Judges and the Judicial Power,* 1985.

Dowrkin, R., *The Law's Empire* 225, 1986, quoted by Upendra Baxi, in *Delhi Law Review,* 13, 1990.

Dr Ambedkar's Contribution to the Indian Economics, Ambedkar Memorial Lectures-II delivered by Pref S. Ambirajan.

Evolution of Provincial Finance in British India, Government of Maharashtra.

Friedmann, W., *Law in a Changing Society,* 1972.

Friedrich, C.J. (Justice), *The Political Act, in Nomos, Justice,* 24 at 34.

Gadekar, *Socio-Economic Thoughts of Ambedkar,* Lucknow.

Gajendragadkar, V.N., "Minority and Backward Community", in *Ambedkar and Social Justice,* Publications Division, Government of India, 1992.

Galanter, Marc, The Abolition of Untouchability — Missed Opportunities : The use and non-use of Law favourable to untouchables and other specially vulnerable Groups. *Law and Society in Modern India,* Oxford: 1992. 208-33.

Galanter, Marc, *Competing Equalities-Law and the Backward Classes in India,* 1984.

Gaskins, Richard, "Second Thoughts on Law as an Instrument of Social Change," *Law and Human Behavior,* 1982, vol. 6, no. 2.

Harivansha Purana.

Harris, J.W., *Legal Philosophies,* London: Butterworth, 1983.

Hart, *The Concept of Law.*

Heggade, O.D., *Economic Thought of Ambedkar.*

Joshi, K.C., "Judicial Process: Recent Trends," *The Journal of Indian Law Institute,* vol. 34, no. 1, 1992.

Joshi, Laxmanshastri, *Tarakateertha Asmila Dasha,* Marathi Quarterly, Diwali Special Issue (1973).

Kamath, H.V., *Constitution Assembly Debates,* vol. 9.

Kamble, N.G., K.M. Kamble, M.L. Kasare (compilor), *Essentials of Dr B.R. Ambedkar,* Nagpur: Social Forum Publications, 1991.

Kasare, M.L., *Economic Philosophy of Ambedkar.*

Kausitaki Grihya-Sutra.

Keer, Dhananjay, *Ambedkar and His Mission.*

Keer, Dhananjay, *Ambedkar — Life and Mission,* Popular Prakashan, Bombay, 1971.

Kharat, Shankarrao, ed., *Letters of Babasaheb Ambedkar,* Marathi edn.

Kosambi, D.D., *Culture and Civilization of Ancient India.*

Kriplani, J.B., *Gandhi — His Life and Thought,* Government of India Publication, 1970.

Krishna Iyer, V.R., *Democracy of Judicial Remedies, a Rejoinder to Hidayatullah,* 4th Sec. 1984.

Krishna Iyer, V.R., *Social Justice, Sunset Dawn,* 2nd edn., 1987.

Krishna Rao, Sivaram, *Relevance of Ambedkarism in India,* ed. K.S. Chalam, Ambedkar's views on Small Holdings in India.

Lokhande, G.H., *Bhimrao Ramji Ambedkar: A Study in Social Democracy,* 1982.

Kumarila Bhatta, *Tantravarttika.*

Mahabharata, Adiparva.

Mungekar, B.L. *Ambedkar on India's Agrarian Problem.*

Rabell, Michael A., "Judicial Activism and the Courts "New Role," *Journal of Social Policy* (USA) Spring, 1982, vol. 12, no. 4.

Raghvendra Rao, K., *Babasaheb Ambedkar: Economic Ideas.*

Rathman, David J., "The Courts and Social Reform" *Law and Human Behavior,* 1982, vol. 6, no. 2.

Report of the Arrears Committee, 1989-90 published by the Supreme Court of India, 1990.

Report of the Backward Classes Commission, vol. I.

Saibaba, G., *"Relevance of Ambedkarism in India",* in K.S. Chalam ed.,

Ambedkar as a Theoretician and Policy Maker.

Sai Baba, Sri Satya, *Sanathan Sarathi,* Prasanthi Nilayam, Anantpur, vol. 21 : 3.

Sashi, S.S., "Collected Works of Dr Ambedkar" in *Ambedkar and Social Justice,* vol. I, Publications Division, Government of India, 1992.

Seervai, H.M., *Constitutional Law of India,* vol. 2.

Seventh Five Year Plan, Planning Commission, Government of India, 1985-90, vol. 11.

Shukla, V.N., *Constitution of India,* 7th edn., 1988.

Singh, Amita, *The Political Philosophy of Betrand Russell,* 1987.

Singh, Parmanand, "Judicial Socialism and Problems of Liberation: Myth and Truth," *Journal of the Indian Law Institute,* vol. 28, no. 3, (July–September 1986).

Stone, *Human Law and Human Justice,* 1948, Meitland Sydney.

The Oxford English Dictionary, vol. VIII, London, 1933.

Tiwari, Rajiv, *Philosophy,* Delhi: Manoj Publications.

Twenty-first Century Universal Encyclopedia, vol. 22.

Vakil, A.K., *Reservation Policy and Scheduled Castes in India,* 1985.

Vibhute, K.I., "Ambedkar's Sense of Social Justice and Constitutional Spirit", *Mainstream,* vol. 31, no. 22, 10 April 1993.

Webster's Third New Dictionary, 1938, vol. II.

Willman, S., *The Principles of Semantics,* 2nd edn., 1957.

Yaska *Nirukta.*

Index